Short Guides to Records

SECOND SERIES

GUIDES 25-48

THE
HISTORICAL
ASSOCIATION

THE VOICE FOR HISTORY

This edition has been edited by **Dr K M Thompson**

The Historical Association was founded in 1906 to bring together people who share an interest in, and love for, the past. The Association still holds these aims. Membership is open to all: teacher and student, amateur and professional. The Historical Association promotes and assists the study of history at all levels to create an environment that supports life long learning. Membership of the Association brings with it big discounts on publications and conferences as well as the subscription magazine of your choice *Teaching History*, *Primary History*, or *The Historian*. Full details are available from *The Historical Association, 59a Kennington Park Road, London SE11 4JH. Telephone: 0171 735 3901. Fax: 0171 582 4989 E-mail: enquiry@history.org.uk*

The publication of a book by the Historical Association does not necessarily imply the Association's approval of the opinions expressed in it.

Acknowledgments: The Historical Association would like to thank the Aurelius Trust for helping to fund the Short Guides in their original leaflet form and also the following members without whom publication of this second volume would not have been possible:

Miss Ursula Pye, Miss Gwendolyn Ivy Fenwick Lennox Gordon, Mr Frederick W. Brooks, Professor Robert L. Zangrando and another member who wishes to remain anonymous.

Design and Production by **Marco Spinelli**

Additional preparation by **Anna Rolfe**

Published by the Historical Association and printed in Great Britain by Blackmore Limited, Longmead, Shaftesbury, Dorset SP7 8PX.

ISBN 085278 406 6

Contents

Introduction 5

Selected Additional Bibliography 7

Churchwardens' Accounts (Short Guide 25) 11

Constables' Accounts (Short Guide 26) 16

Overseers' Accounts (Short Guide 27) 21

Settlement Papers (Short Guide 28) 25

Apprenticship and Bastardy Records (Short Guide 29) 29

Parish Registers (Short Guide 30) 33

Archdeacons' Records (Short Guide 31) 38

Bishops' Registers (Short Guide 32) 44

The 1669 Return of Nonconformist Conventicles (Short Guide 33) 50

Probate Accounts (Short Guide 34) 55

Census Returns in England and Wales (Short Guide 35) 59

The Lloyd George Finance Act Material (Short Guide 36) 62

Assistant Poor Law Commissioners' Correspondance (Short Guide 37) 70

Pipe Rolls (Short Guide 38) 75

Building Plans (Short Guide 39) 79

Ordnance Survey Maps (Short Guide 40) 83

Aerial Photography for Archaeology (Short Guide 41) 87

Canal & Railway Plans (Short Guide 42) 93

Fire Insurance Plans (Short Guide 43) 98

School Log Books (Short Guide 44) 104

The 1851 Religious Census (Short Guide 45) 109

Coroners' Inquest Records (Short Guide 46) 114

Manorial Court Rolls (Short Guide 47) 118

Prison Registers and Prison Hulk Records (Short Guide 48) 123

Introduction
to second series

Since Lionel Munby edited the first series of *Short Guides to Records* and wrote its introduction in 1972 much has happened on the local history scene. The original set of 24 titles was published between 1961 and 1971 in *History* and was only terminated as a result of a change in editorial policy. A lot of obvious subjects had not been covered and it was therefore decided to produce a further 24 titles to fill these omissions. Publication has been possible thanks to a generous grant from the Aurelius Trust whose help is warmly acknowledged.

It is not an exaggeration to say that there has been an explosion in local history activity in the last 25 years. At the academic level several universities now offer certificates, diplomas and higher degrees in the subject and at least one also runs a BA degree course. An important landmark was the publication of the report of the Committee to Review Local History (chaired by Lord Blake) in 1979 which led to the establishment of the British Association for Local History in 1982. This new body received generous financial assistance in its first three years which enabled it to appoint a field officer, whose role was to discover the amount and type of local history activity in the country at large. David Hayns' reports are a fascinating snapshot and include detailed studies of a number of counties.

BALH also took over responsibility for *The Local Historian*, which had started life in 1952 as The *Amateur Historian*. It remains the preeminent academic journal and there is no slackening in the quantity and quality of material submitted to its editor. Another national publication, *Local History Magazine*, began life in 1984. The Historical Association's quarterly magazine, *The Historian*, usually contains one local history article. At the sub-national level local history titles proliferate: most counties in England and Wales have a county-wide journal and in addition there are hundreds of titles covering smaller areas. These vary in sophistication, quality and frequency and many have benefited from the availability of relatively cheap desktop publishing packages.

Another new initiative which has spread across the country like wildfire is the local history fair. These first appeared in the early 1980s and have since been held all over the British Isles. They range from one-county affairs held for a day to regional activities lasting for a weekend. They bring together local historians and others interested in the past, and usually contain a mixture of historical re-enactments, displays by local societies and bookstalls. The more popular events, such as the Essex fairs, attract thousands of people and even in the winter there is at least one local history event held somewhere in the country every week. The British Association for Local History published a guide in 1989, *Running a local history fair* by Vic Gray and Bill Liddell.

At the grass-roots level interest in local history has mushroomed. The Historical Association has long had a network of local branches, some of which have been very active in research and publication. Many talks to HA branches have a local history theme. There are hundreds of local history societies, varying in size and activity, as well as specialist societies. Most counties in England and

Wales have an 'umbrella' organisation which co-ordinates activity in its area. Much of the increased interest in local history has stemmed from the family history 'boom'. Many adults were attracted to history through a desire to know more about their own antecedents and it is a logical next step to wish to understand the kind of lives lived by their ancestors. Many family historians have 'moved on' to local history and some very worthy research has resulted.

Both family and local historians have undertaken much research that has helped others. The family historians in particular have been very active in producing indexes to popular records such as the census returns and poor law papers, which has the additional benefit of reducing wear and tear on original records. All of this activity has put pressure on record offices which has caused short-term problems. However most archivists welcome this increased use, as evidence of the value placed on their services by an growing number of local tax payers. A number of 'Friends of Record Offices' have been formed from the Public Record Office downwards; at the national level the National Council on Archives brings together professional bodies, such as the Society of Archivists and the Association of Chief Archivists in Local Government, and user groups, such as the Federation of Family History Societies, the British Association for Local History and the Historical Association. Public support for record offices has been impressive and it is clear that attempts to curtail archive services will meet with very vocal resistance.

The efforts of archivists and others have introduced local historians to previously unknown sources for research. It is now much easier to get information on the whereabouts of different types of records and the second series of *Short Guides* will help in this process. The number of instructional books for local historians has blossomed since Lionel Munby wrote his introduction to the first series and a new bibliography accompanies the second series. There are a number of specialist publishers, such as Phillimore and Alan Sutton, who sell textbooks and studies of individual places and subjects for the whole country. Other publishers specialise in a particular region or subject and many of the major firms now include some local history titles in their lists. In addition the Historical Association, the British Association for Local History and the Federation of Family History Societies all produce short pamphlets and occasionally longer works on the subject. BALH for example has published two educational books for schools: *The Late Victorian Town* and *The Union Workhouse*, with the help of the Gulbenkian Foundation.

The editor and authors of this new series of *Short Guides* hope that their efforts will help local historians in their research.

Kate Thompson

Selected Additional Bibliography: Addenda

In the reprinted *Short Guides to Records, First series* (1994) there is a 'Selected Additional Bibliography' (pp. 9-14) which lists the numerous useful works on archives, sources and methods published since the original *Short Guides* were issued; the following *Addenda* supplement that list.

DIRECTORIES AND GENERAL GUIDES TO ARCHIVE COLLECTIONS

(i) Directories

Foster, J and Sheppard, J, *British Archives: a guide to archive resources in the United Kingdom* (3rd edn, Macmillan, 1995)

(ii) General Guides to Archives

Royal Commission on Historical Manuscripts, publications: *Guides to Sourcesfor British History.* (HMSO) include family and estate collections, family names A-K [L-Y forthcoming];

Surveys of Historical Manuscripts in the United Kingdom (HMSO, 3rd edn, 1997).

Public Record Office: Current Guide (PRO, 1996)

Olney, RJ, *Manuscript Sources for British History* (Institute of Historical Research, University of London, 1995)

Wallis, H and McConnell, A (eds) *Historians' Guide to Early British Maps* (Royal Historical Society Guides and Handbooks, no. 18, 1994)

Printed historical records: Stevenson, D and Stevenson, W, *Scottish Texts and Calendars: an analytical guide to serial publications* (Royal Historical Society Guides and Handbooks, no. 14, 1987)

GUIDES TO SOURCES AND METHODS

(i) Sources: General

Moody, D, *Scottish Local History: an introductory guide* (Batsford, 1986)

Sinclair, C, *Tracing Scottish Local History* (HMSO, 1994)

(ii) Methods and the Use of Sources: General

Drake, M and Finnegan, R (eds) *Sources and Methods for Family and Community Historians: a handbook*

(iii) Guides to Specific Sources

Alvey, N, *From Chantry to Oxfam: a short history of charities and charity legislation* (British Association for Local History, 1996)

Bruce. A. *Monuments, Memorials and the Local Historian* (Historical Association, 1997)

Caunce, S, *Oral History and the Local Historian* (Batsford, 1994)

Ellis, M, *Using Manorial Records* (Public Record Office, 1994)

Evans, E J and Crosby, A G, *Tithes, Maps, Apportionments and the 1836 Act* (British Association for Local History, 3rd edn, 1997)

Federation of Family History Societies, publications ed. Gibson, JSW and others, include: census returns; local newspapers; probate jurisdictions; quarter sessions records; poll books; land tax assessments; coroners' records; electoral registers; hearth tax; muster rolls and militia lists; poor law union records

Foster, D, *The Rural Constabulary Act 1839* (British Association for Local History, 1982)

Friar,S, *Heraldry for the Local Historian and Genealogist* (Sutton, 1996)

Gaskell, S M, *Building Control: National Legislation and the Introduction of Local Byelaws* (British Association for Local History, 1983)

Glennie, P, *Distinguishing Men's Trades, occupational sources and debates for pre-Census England* (Historical Geography Research Series, no. 25, Institute of British Geographers, 1990)

Hoyle, R W, *Tudor Taxation Records* (Public Record Office, 1994)

Machin, B, *Rural Housing: an historical approach* (Historical Association, 1994)

Morgan, P, *Domesday Book and the Local Historian* (Historical Association, 1994)

Perks, R, *Oral History* (Historical Association, 2nd edn, 1995)

Pooley, C G, *Local Authority Housing* (Historical Association, 1996)

Reed, M (ed) *Discovering Past Landscapes* (Croom Helm, 1984)

Schurer, K, and Arkell (eds) *Surveying the People* (Local Population Studies Supplement, 1992)

Shorney, D, *Protestant Nonconformity and Roman Catholicism* (Public Record Office, 1996)

Swift, R, *The Irish in Britain 1815-1914* (Historical Association, 1990)

Tarver, A, *Church Court Records* (Phillimore, 1994)

Watts, M R, *The Chapel and the National: Nonconformity and the local historian* (Historical Association, 1996)

West, J, *Village Records* (Phillimore, 3rd edn, 1997)

REFERENCE

Currie, C R J and Lewis, C P (eds) *English County Histories: a guide* (Sutton, 1994)

Field, J, A *History of English Field Names* (Longman, 1993)

Gelling, M, *Signposts to the Past* (Phillimore, 3rd edn, 1997)

Hey, D (ed) *The Oxford Companion to Local and Family History* (Oxford U.P. 1996)

Hey, D, *The Oxford Dictionary of Local and Family History* (Oxford U.P. 1997)

Horn, JM, *History Theses, 1981-90* (Institute of Historical Research, University of London,1994)

McKinley, R A, A *History of British Surnames* (Longman, 1990)

Mills, A D, A *Dictionary of English Place-Names* (Oxford U.P. 199 1)

Munby, L, *How Much is That Worth.?* (British Association for Local History, 2nd edn,1996)

Munby, L, *Timing and Dating: a handbook for local historians* (British Association for Local History, 1997)

Stuart, D, *Latin for Local and Family Historians* (Phillimore, 1995)

G.C.F.Forster

Churchwardens' Accounts

David Dymond

EXTRACTS DRAWN FROM DIFFERENT PLACES AND PERIODS

(Sources: J. C. Cox, *Churchwardens' Accounts* and original accounts for Boxford and Mendlesham in Suffolk Record Office.)

St Margaret, Southwark, 1453/4: 'Peid for a pley upon Seynt Lucy day, and for a pley upon Seynt Margrete day, 13s. 4d.'

Yatton, Somerset, 1481: 'Paide att Bristowe [Bristol] for a sewte of vestments and a cope, £26' [*sic*].

Walberswick, Suffolk, 1496: 'By a gadering of the wyvys in the towne for a glaswyndow, 9s.'

Bassingbourne, Cambs., 1497/8: 'Rec' att the fryste [first] may ale, and all charges borne, 18s. 2d.'

St Edmund, Salisbury, 1511: 'Of Master Chasey for the hire of xx shepe wiche John Ludlow did geve to the mayntenyng of Seynt Sebastians light, 6s.'

Ashburton, Devon, 1538/9: For painting the south part of the roodloft ... £16 13s. 4d. 1547/8: For taking down the rood and other images, 3s. 4d.

1554/5: 'For mending of the rode loft, 6d.'

1563/4: 'For pullyng downe of the roode loufte, 2s. 8d.'

St Mary, Reading, 1557: 'Payed to the minstrelles and the hobby horse uppon May day, 3s.'

St Martin, Leicester, 1562/3: 'Payd for wyne for the Communeon at Estur iij quartes of mamse [malmsey] and ix quartes of claret wyne, 4s. 6d.'

Mendlesham, Suffolk, 1593: 'At Berri [Bury St Edmunds] at the bisshops visytacion for our booke of artyckells, 6d.'

1603: 'Layd out for Elsabeth Morwell hur buryall, for hur shete, hur keper, hur bearers and other charges to the sexten, 5s. 8d.'

1605: '...for glasyng the churche and chansell, £2 11s. 0d.'

1610: ' More to hym [the sexten] for fraunkensence to burn in the churche at two tymes, 4d.'

... For 'jemmers and two lockes and keys for two chestes mad in the stoles in the chauncell for the scolmaster and scollers to lock up ther bookes, paper, ynk and other necessaryes, 3s. 2d.'

1614: 'Layd out to George Campe his wife, for cakes and bere at Mellis Greene for the soldiers that served then for the towne, 2s. 8d.

... More given to Christopher Ship his wife, in regard that shee hath taken home hir childe and nurced it hirselfe, she and hire houshould beinge yet visited with sicknes, 4s.'

... To Widow Cunold 'in great extremity', 12d.

St Petrock, Exeter, 1633: 'For a book lately set forth for recreatyon, 6d.' [James I's controversial 'Book of Sports', re-issued by Charles I]

Boxford, Suffolk, 1702: 'For sack to cause such a number of females to drink, as disencompass [*sic*] the church and steeple round, 12s. 6d.'

St Mary, Warwick, 1815/6: 'Paid to the ringers for news of the battle of Waterloo, £2 2s.; ditto for taking of Bonaparte, £1 11s. 6d.'

ORIGIN

Churchwardens, who were normally men but occasionally women, were the principal lay officers of ecclesiastical parishes. They were local residents elected or appointed annually, usually by the joint decision of incumbent and people, and received expenses but rarely any pay. Their origins go back to a time, broadly between the twelfth and fourteenth centuries, when the laity were assuming new responsibilities for gathering money and other resources, furnishing liturgical equipment for the whole church (including the rector's chancel), and maintaining the fabric of the nave. In the Middle Ages they were known under alternative titles such as guardians, church-reeves, proctors and *yconomi,* which emphasize their role as providers and custodians entrusted with the corporate property of the whole parish. They should not be confused with other small groups of principal inhabitants known for example as 'the Four Men' who wielded authority on matters of general policy. Generally two wardens acted concurrently, but in large upland parishes with many scattered townships and hamlets, the number could be as high as twelve. Holders of this prestigious office were expected to be honest, capable, economically 'substantial' and already experienced at a lower level of public affairs. In practice they were often middling people of 'the better sort' (but usually below the rank of gentry), for example yeoman, clothiers and shopkeepers. Although some people were keen to avoid this demanding voluntary job, others served more than once—for consecutive years or at intervals.

The range of duties was indeed onerous. For example, by the Canons of 1604 the ecclesiastical duties of churchwardens included maintaining the church and churchyard; providing all necessary furnishings such as communion table, poor-box and large bible; buying sufficient quantities of bread and wine for communion; preventing any profane actions in or around the church; ensuring that parishioners attended church regularly; keeping a record of visiting preachers; and with questmen and minister presenting offences at the visitations of archdeacon and bishop. In the last resort they were the eyes and ears of the local bishop, responsible for reporting any backsliding by parishioners or clergy. Other duties of a secular kind were imposed on them by statute from the reign of Henry VIII onwards. For instance they had to enforce the wearing of English woollen caps and the destruction of vermin, pay for the arming and training of local militiamen, and share in the work of highway surveyors and overseers of the poor.

So their varied work brought churchwardens into contact with the incumbent and other local clergy, with archdeacons, bishops and their legal representatives, with magistrates, with several other local officials both ecclesiastical and secular, and finally with all kinds of parishioner from gentleman to pauper. No other local official was of such crucial importance in husbanding the burgeoning wealth of the late-medieval parish, or in implementing the detailed orders of higher authority during the various stages of the Reformation. Indeed the churchwarden remained a figure of prime significance in the local community until the nineteenth century when governmental reforms progressively destroyed the autonomy of the old parish—a process which culminated in the creation of purely secular Parish Councils in 1894.

LOCATION AND FORMAT

Traditionally churchwardens' accounts, whether bound or loose, were kept in the parish chest. Over the centuries many have unfortunately perished so that only a small proportion survives today. For example, Suffolk with over 500 medieval parishes now has only 43 sets of churchwardens' accounts for the sixteenth and seventeenth centuries, and few of those are consecutive for more than 40 years. The accounts of small rural parishes, as opposed to larger villages and market towns, are particularly rare. Proportionally more accounts survive from the eighteenth and nineteenth centuries, but their scope is usually limited to the maintainance and equipment of the church and lacks the broader social and administrative dimensions of former times. Nowadays, most surviving accounts of any date are in the professional care of county or diocesan record offices. Some accounts have been published, at least partially, by individual local historians or by record societies; most of these cover the period from the fifteenth to seventeenth centuries and some, it must be confessed, contain alarming inaccuracies.

Earlier medieval accounts are in Latin, but English took over generally during the fifteenth century. Each year the wardens, either separately or together, drew up accounts of the parish's total income and expenditure. These they presented for public audit at a parish meeting or vestry, which was held at various times but mainly came to be associated with Easter. Income could come from several sources such as voluntary collections or 'gatherings', fees for burials, bequests, hirings of animals belonging to the parish, rents of land and other property such as town houses, rents of pews, church rates which were not abolished until 1867, or money-raising events like plays, church-ales and wakes. Details of expenditure were based on earlier bills and receipts which usually have not survived. However, it should be noted that the actual form and content of this class of document are highly variable. Sometimes the accounts of other subsidiary fund-holders are included, and some so-called churchwardens' accounts were in fact kept by clergy. Furthermore, in books or bundles labelled 'churchwardens' accounts', the historian may find other kinds of record like lists of church goods, bede rolls, accounts of poor relief and local charities, briefs, annual lists of elected officers, and major decisions of the vestry.

As with all kinds of account, historians will meet many frustrations such as insufficient detail, lumping together information in vague phrases like '. . . and other necessaries', and uncertainty as to who was actually being paid. Nor is it enough, as Charles Drew warned long ago, to read what is actually contained in an account, 'unless one has also a certain knowledge of what might be expected to be there, and is not'. Care must also be taken to distinguish different kinds of entry: routine, occasional and one-off. The stock payments include providing bread and wine for communion, maintaining bells, washing surplices and attending visitations: these are the repetitive but significant rhythms of parish life which, in the words of John Craig, provide a 'thick layer of information against which the oft deceptive records of the courts or rhetoric of the clergy can be properly contextualized'. Such entries generally show an understandable conformity and deference to the constant stream of instructions issuing from bishops, parliament or the crown. Occasionally, however, the historian can find statements which hint at local independence, internal conflict or parochial policies tending towards the radical or conservative extremes. Thus Craig argued that the sale of organs and purchase of a Geneva bible in the 1580s at Mildenhall (Suffolk) indicate puritan influence, while Eamon Duffy has pointed to an entry in the accounts of Morebath (Devon), long in print but formerly overlooked, which could mean that this deeply conservative parish sent men to fight in the western rebellion of 1549.

USES

Over several generations historians have used churchwardens' accounts to throw light on a wide range of subjects. Traditional interests have included the physical fabric of churches, especially their remodelling and rebuilding in the fifteenth and early sixteenth centuries, and their equipping and beautification (by means of vestments, plate, service books, lights and much else). Both these medieval initiatives were largely funded by the laity. Another important issue has been the detailed and often costly implementation of the Reformation and Counter-Reformation, for example how features such as rood-screens, stone altars and images were removed in the reign of Edward VI, only to be restored under Queen Mary.

In recent years research has become more analytical and shifted to new themes such as the intricacies of parochial finance; the balance between lay and clerical involvement; the development of puritan 'iconophobia'; and the attempt to impose a much stricter personal and social morality in the later sixteenth and early seventeenth centuries. Detailed but highly significant aspects of local life have been recovered from churchwardens' accounts like the purchase of more than one quality of communion wine; the evolving calendar of official celebrations, both Catholic and Protestant; intensification of timekeeping by means of bells and clocks; the fashion of change-ringing; the enjoyment of drama, sports, ales, revels and other customary recreations; and education by means of schools or personal tuition. New work is also in progress on the sorts of people who became churchwarden, how effective they were in coping with pressures from above and below, and how in dealing with their neighbours they juggled with the competing principles of 'co-operation' and 'coercion'. Examples have been found of churchwardens who failed in their duties and in their personal behaviour; some even belonged to heretical groups such as the Lollards and Family of Love. In other words, the emphasis is now much more obviously on the dynamics and politics of individual parishes, and how they varied. From all parts of the country there are hundreds of churchwardens' accounts which at best have only been picked over or glanced at. Much more serious analysis and comparison need to be done if we are to extract full value from these wide-ranging sources, and thereby understand better the vital and subtle interplay of local and national life.

BIBLIOGRAPHY

Aston, M, 'Iconoclasm at Rickmansworth, 1522: Troubles of Churchwardens' in Aston, M, (ed.), *Faith and Fire: Popular and Unpopular Religion, 1350-1600* (1993), pp.231-60.

Burgess, C, *The Pre-Reformation Records of All Saints', Bristol* (Bristol Record Society, 1995).

Carlson, E, 'The Origins, Function and Status of the Office of Churchwarden, with Particular Reference to the Diocese of Ely' in Spufford, M, (ed.), *The World of Rural Dissenters, 1520-1725* (Cambridge, 1995), pp.164-207.

Collinson, P, *From Iconoclasm to Iconophobia: the Cultural Impact of the Second English Reformation* (Reading, 1986).

Cox, J C, *Churchwardens' Accounts from the Fourteenth Century to the Close of the Seventeenth Century (1913).* Lists published and unpublished churchwardens' accounts in Chapter III and Addenda (p.353).

Craig, J S, 'Co-operation and Initiatives: Elizabethan Churchwardens and the Parish Accounts of Mildenhall', *Social History*, 18, No.3 (Oct.,1993), 357-80.

Craig, J S & Kumin, B, *English Churchwardens and the Parish, 1350-1700* (forthcoming).

Cressy, D, *Bonfires and Bells: National Memory and the Protestant Calendar in Elizabethan and Stuart England* (1989).

Drew, D, *Lambeth Churchwardens' Accounts, 1504-1645* (Surrey Record Society, 1941), Introduction, pp.x-lvi.

Duffy, E, *The Stripping of the Altars* (Yale, 1992).

Foster, J E, *Churchwardens' Accounts of St Mary the Great, Cambridge, from 1504 to 1635* (Cambridge Antiquarian Society, 1905).

Hutton, R, 'The Local Impact of the Tudor Reformations' in Haigh, C, (ed.), *The English Reformation Revised* (CUP, 1987).

Hutton, R, *The Rise and Fall of Merry England* (Oxford, 1994). Lists all surviving churchwardens' accounts before 1690 in Appendix, pp.263-93.

Kumin, B A, *The Shaping of a Community: The Rise and Reformation of the English Parish, c. 1400 - 1560* (Scolar Press, 1996).

Morrill, J, 'The Church in England, 1642-9' in Morrill, J, (ed.), *Reactions to the English Civil War, 1642-9*, (1982).

Records of Early English Drama (Univ. of Toronto Press, 1979 onwards). Volumes on individual counties and major towns, publishing evidence of 'dramatic, ceremonial and minstrel activity in Gt Britain before 1642'.

Swayne, H J F, *Churchwardens' Accounts of St Edmund and St Thomas, Sarum, 1443 - 1702* (Wiltshire Record Society, 1896).

Tate, W E, *The Parish Chest* (CUP, 1960), pp.83-107.

Whiting, R, *The Blind Devotion of the People* (CUP, 1989).

Wright, S J, (ed.), *Parish, Church and People: Local Studies in Lay Religion, 1350-1750*, (1988).

Wrightson, K, 'The Politics of the Parish in Early Modern England' in Griffiths, P, Fox, A, and Hindle, S, (eds) *The Experience of Authority in Early Modern England* (Basingstoke: Macmillan, 1996), pp. 10 - 46.

26
Constables' Accounts
Martyn Bennett

[FROM THE BRANSTON CONSTABLES' ACCOUNTS 1611-1676, LEICESTERSHIRE COUNTY RECORD OFFICE DE720/30.]

John Newton accounts, Branston, 1615

Imprimis payed unto Maister Jackson for meamed souldiers and hospitals for Easter quarter	iis	
Item for towe men charges when the where at Leicestr be fore the Justices	iis	xd
Item payed unto Maister Jackson for pultree	vs	
Item payed unto Maister Jackson for a benevolence for our King	vis	id
Item payed when where before the Justices at Melton for the pore for our charges	iiis	
Item payed unto the chiefeconstable for meamed soldiers and hostpitals for Trinite quarter	iis	
Item payed unto two poore men w[i]th a pasport	iiiid	

[FROM UPTON CONSTABLES' ACCOUNTS, NOTTINGHAMSHIRE ARCHIVE OFFICE, PR 1710]

The Layings forth of Jane Kitchen Widowe shee hiring one to serve the Constables office this present yeare 1644 as followeth.

Imprimis spent upon Plowmundy	2	3
Item given to Edward Kooe for going with a troope to Burton by Gensborrow		8
spent at the Leete when I tooke my oath		6
payed to Mr Oglethorp for a payre of boots for a souldier	2	
spent when the Souldiers kept the courte of garde at George Houghton his house	7	
spent at Kerkes when the quarter Masters were writing the Billittes	1	2

THE OFFICE OF CONSTABLE

The petty constable was the oldest of the parish officers, being recorded as early as the thirteenth century. The office had its origins in pre-conquest society and was derived from the position of 'headman' or 'executive officer' of a village community. By at least the sixteenth century the constable was chosen annually within the community, by election from the town or village hierarchy, or by houserow in which all the major landholders took a turn. However the origin of the office lay in manorial administration and the person chosen had to be confirmed by the court leet, in some parts of the country until 1842. As shown in the second extract, the first entry in the constable's account book often referred to his or her selection by fellow parishioners but the inhabitants of a parish never acquired the legal right to interfere with his selection or appointment. From 1842 the constable was appointed by the vestry until the office disappeared in 1889 when the newly formed County Councils took over his duties.

The constable's immediate superior was the High or Chief Constable who was responsible for the hundred in which the constablewick lay. For much of his time in office, the constable was a servant of the county justices of the peace: he had to execute their warrants and obey their orders, and attend them at petty or quarter sessions. The justices administered the oath of office to constables and were able to replace unsuitable or impoverished ones. The constable had to inform each quarter session of the state of his village, by means of a presentment dealing with the keeping of the peace, the state of the poor and the condition of the roads passing through the constablewick; he could be fined for not supplying this information. As the constable was not a parish officer *per se* the way in which his expenses were paid before 1778 is obscure although in 1662 Parliament empowered a parish rate to be levied for his expenses connected with vagrancy. His origin as an officer of the manor is reflected in the alternative titles of headborough, thirdborough, verderer, borsholder, tithingman or chief pledge.

The constable had a large number of duties, not all of which he was able to perform. He was responsible for looking after the welfare of the parish bull; supervising the pinfold and stocks; providing and maintaining the parish butts, and making sure they were properly used; and taking charge of the parish armour. He assisted the churchwardens in ensuring attendance at church and convened parish meetings when necessary. As he was responsible to the Lord Lieutenant and his deputies, from the 1580s onwards the constable had to manage the parish's contribution, in men and money, to the militia, at their behest. He also had to collect the county rate and summon the coroner's jury.

The constable's policing duties included responsibility for appointing watch and ward within the village or town from 1285; he also had to raise a hue and cry to pursue felons and convey villagers charged with appearing at the quarter sessions or assizes. He had the power to apprehend anyone found guilty of a crime or who was likely to cause a breach of the peace. Until the end of the sixteenth century he was responsible for beggars, the lodging of the impotent poor and the apprenticing of children. These duties were later transferred to either the churchwardens or overseers of the poor but the constable was responsible for the administration of the Vagrancy Acts and the supervision of ale-houses until about 1700. He had the responsibility for whipping vagrants, unmarried mothers and putative fathers in the community; vagrants and those who harboured them had to be reported by the constable who was also responsible for taking care of travellers with passes. Alewives were taken to the Assizes of Ales by the constable, who also had to ensure that only licensed premises sold ale, and that all weights, measures and vessels conformed to regulations. The constable also regulated excise payments from the civil war period onwards.

The shrievalty imposed numerous duties on the constable, many involving the collection of taxes. The constable and a meeting of 'neighbours' set the rates to be paid and the constable and deputies were responsible for collecting them. Monies were often paid to the chief constable for such things as benevolences for the monarch, pensions for maimed soldiers, money for the upkeep of hospitals and gaols and (in the seventeenth century) Ship Money, Coat and Conduct money and the Hearth Tax. Other responsibilities included the appointment of a surveyor of the roads and the maintenance of them. The constable also had to levy horses and or wagons from the constablewicks for the use of the Postmaster or the saltpetre-men working in the gunpowder industry. As well as national taxes the constable could charge the cost of the office via the levying of lewns (a locally assessed rate, such as that collected by churchwardens for the church rate); partly in order to facilitate this the practice of keeping a set of accounts developed and was formalised in the 1660s.

THE LOCATION OF THE RECORDS

Unfortunately only a very few account books seem to have survived. Many records may only have been kept on loose papers which were re-used, lost or destroyed when the accounts had been audited. Some sets of constables' papers include only copies of warrants, others only rating lists. It is rare to find a full set of papers including not only these but the full details of income and disbursements. Many of the papers were destroyed or re-used after their audit when the totals and balance were entered in the Town Book. They were recorded on paper, sometimes bound as a Town Book with the accounts of the churchwardens and overseers of the poor. Like other accounts of the same period Roman numerals were often used at first but from the 1630s the transition to arabic numbers began.

Accounts follow the general pattern shown in the extracts with the money recorded on the right of the page. On the left hand side were the names of the people levied or the items for which the constable had disbursed money. However some accounts are only fragmentary, recording only total outlay or income, and this may occur within an otherwise full set of accounts. The account books were latterly stored in the parish chest but there is evidence of constables retaining their own records. In some parishes the accounts may remain in the parish and permission to see them must be obtained in the usual way. However most constables' accounts are now deposited in county record offices where they will be listed with other parish records. Other accounts may be found in the Public Record Office or the British Library.

THE USES OF THE RECORDS

In recent years a reassessment of the role of the constable has been carried out. This has redefined the nature of the office and the efficiency with which it was conducted. Traditional views of the inefficiency of the village official owed a lot to Shakespeare's constable Dogberry, in *Much Ado about Nothing*, and historians who saw the post being filled by the 'idiotic', the 'infirm' and the incapable. The office has instead been identified as onerous and filled by hardworking unpaid people drawn from the small farming husbandman class, yeomen and perhaps the lower gentry depending on the town or village social structure. Recent work on Norfolk communities has suggested that churchwardens ranked higher in society than the constables. However, it would seem that generally the two officials were people of the same status. Moreover, there would seem to be a pool of 'neighbours' in each community, of roughly equal social standing which provided all the officers of the community, constables, overseers of the poor, churchwardens and the auditors of accounts. The use of the constable's records and associated documents from the parish, such as registers and the accounts of other officials, enables the reconstruction of communities as dynamic social structures. The function of the hierarchy and the taxpaying community can be traced, as can their relationship to broader parish society. The economic and social forces of the communities are also revealed in the accounts, due to the constable being responsible for the regulation of trade and of the poor law. A constable's regard for law and order, the supervision of travellers and the apprehension of vagrants gives us a picture of the town and village in the wider sphere of the region and the nation, during peace, war, plagues and dearth.

Recent work has placed the constable at the heart of local government. The increasing centralisation of government can be examined as the office of constable became increasingly absorbed into the county power structure. The operation of military affairs, financial affairs and legal matters can be examined as the tentacles of government stretched downward via the constables into the villages. Studies have revealed that there may have existed two concepts of social order, one held by the governing class of which the constable was a tool, and another by the wider community of the governed of whom the constable was a representative. This led to conflict, especially in the area of the law and social peace, with the constable in the dichotomous position of serving two masters with conflicting views.

For the period of the civil wars in the 1640s and 1650s, account books reveal clearly the structure of the administrations of the rival factions. They show that towns and villages were subjected to the collection of high levels of taxation, and the constant requisitioning of materials such as beds, bedding, fuels, timber, wagons, horses and labour. They provide an invaluable aid to the understanding of the function of the war efforts in the civil war, enabling the war to be seen beyond the confines of battles and sieges.

Finally, the account books provide witting and unwitting testimony to the role of women in village and town society. Women are shown operating in the market place as traders and consumers, providing money and provisions to constables at various times. They can clearly be seen in the brewing side of the agricultural community dealing with the justices over regulations on ale production and in the retail side in the position as 'alewives'. Occasionally a woman, most probably a widow, could serve as a constable when the system of selection was by houserow, which made serving unavoidable. In such instances, as with the excerpt above, a substitute had to be hired to fulfill the functions of the office which entailed dealing with higher ranking officers of government, especially the justices of the peace, who would have been unlikely to administer an oath to a woman. Nevertheless it is likely that Jane Kitchen would have borne responsibility for the general running of the office of constable albeit in a somewhat restricted way.

BIBLIOGRAPHY

Bennett, Martyn, ed., *A Nottinghamshire Village in War and Peace: The Accounts of the Constables of Upton 1640 - 1660*, (1995)

Fletcher, Anthony, *Reform in the Provinces*, (1985)

Fox, Levi, ed., *Coventry Constables' Presentments*, (1986)

Gardiner, Robert, *The Compleat Constable*, (1700)

Kent, Joan, 'The English Village Constable, 1580-1642; The Nature and Dilemmas of the Office', (*The Journal of British Studies*, XX, No 2, 1981)

Kent, Joan, *The English Village Constable: 1580-1642*, (1986)

Price, F D, ed., *The Wigginton Constables' Book,* (1971)

Roberts, Stephen, *Restoration and Reaction*, Devon Local Administration, (1984)

Tate, W E, *The Parish Chest*, (3rd edn, 1969, reprinted 1983)

Wrightson, Keith, 'Two Concepts of order: justices, constables and jurymen in seventeenth century England' in Brewer, J and Styles J, *An Ungovernable People*, (1983)

Webb, Sidney and Beatrice, *English Local Government from the Revolution to the Municipal Corporations Act: The parish and the county*, (1906)

Overseers' Accounts
G W Oxley

Extracts from the overseers' accounts for the parish of Culham, Oxfordshire for the year 1780-1 (Oxfordshire Record Office DD par Culham b5)

April 29 One week pay to following persons

Roses children		3	
Martha Pithouse	3		
Wm. White for Huntingtons children	3		
Mary Brooks for Everets child	2		
Wm. Collins		2	6
Thos Everat		2	
Henry Dew		2	
Widow Honey		1	6
Sarah Wase		1	6

Extracts from the overseers' accounts for the parish of Aughton, Lancashire for the year 1771-2 (Lancashire Record Office, PR58)

Spent at entering office	1		
for coverlids & blankets for Elizabeth Nelson	9		
To Alice Nelson for relief	1		
To Elizabeth Hatton for Sutherns wife children		18	6
To Alice Nelson in sickness		2	
To 2 smocks for Widow Smalley	4	6	
Spent at a Vestry Meeting		1	
expences concerning Alice Hilton's bastard child		4	
To leading a load of coals for Alice Houghton	1	1	
To mending Twists childrens shoes		7	
for filling a bed with chaff for Eliza Nelson	1		
To Elizabeth Halton for the cure of the bite of a mad dog		2	
Paid towards the Funeral Expences of Mars Poaket		6	9
Paid Doctor Aspinwall	2	2	

ORIGIN

Overseers' accounts are the core record of the parochial administration of poor relief which operated in England and Wales from the early seventeenth century to the 1830s. Towards the end of the sixteenth century poor relief and the taxation to finance it was administered on a voluntary basis under permissive legislation or as a local initiative in response to a particular problem. The whole system was codified and made compulsory by the Poor Law Act of 1601 but there was a considerable time lapse before it was fully implemented in the more remote parts of the country. Under the 1601 Act each parish was required to appoint annually two of its ratepayers as overseers of the poor. They were unpaid and the office usually rotated round the members of the parish elite. Their duties were to raise money by means of rates levied on the occupiers of property and to relieve the poor in the ways set down in the Act. At the end of their year of office they were required to set down all their transactions in a set of accounts for audit by their fellow parishioners and approval by the local magistrate.

FORMAT AND CONTEXT

Provided that these simple requirements were met there were no regulations as to how the accounts should be set out. The only specific requirement was imposed in the 1690s and required the inclusion of a list of the parish pensioners, i.e. those who were being permanently maintained out of the rates. All accounts have a broad similarity simply because of the limited range of items to be included but it does not follow that all accounts look alike. In practice, local customs developed so that the accounts of neighbouring parishes have obvious similarities but appear quite different from those produced in a distant part of the country. It must also be remembered that, except in the larger or wealthier parishes where paid staff were employed, the accounts were compiled by a different person every year. Thus it is possible to find well set out accounts in beautiful copperplate for one year followed by a scrappy, ill written, ill spelt, attempt the next. Behind the local variations three main elements can usually be discerned. The statutory list of the poor usually appears, sometimes once at the beginning of the account, sometimes at regular intervals recording the payments actually made. The second and usually the largest element are the one-off payments to the poor. They relate to both extraordinary payments for the regular poor, whose names appear in the list of pensioners, and to occasional payments to others who were financially independent under normal circumstances but were obliged to resort to public funds for unusual or unexpected expenditure. The disbursements could relate to any aspect of living expenses but rent, clothing, fuel, and medical expenses were among the most common. The third and least important element comprised payments of administrative expenses. These included costs incurred at meetings, expenditure incurred on journeys to magistrates to obtain signatures to accounts and appointments or seeking adjudications and orders in connection with bastardy or settlement and removal, and legal expenses.

USES

Overseers' accounts may be used for several distinct but related types of enquiry.

Firstly and most directly they are the primary source for the investigation of the way in which the system of poor relief itself operated and evolved. Through a long run of accounts we can trace the emergence of different types of relief such as the use of medical services or workhouses. In the records of rural parishes in the south of England we can pinpoint the emergence of the roundsman system as a means of dealing with unemployment and a precursor of the Speenhamland response to the harvest failures from 1795 onwards. In the accounts of the early nineteenth century we may trace the problems which eventually overwhelmed the parochial system of relief. On the one hand are the desperate expedients adopted by overseers in the country parishes to cope with the structural unemployment which arose when population was growing steadily while the economic base was static or contracting. On the other hand were the equally daunting problems experienced by their counterparts in the industrial areas as a result of mass destitution associated with cyclical unemployment or the creeping impoverishment of workers whose skills were replaced by mechanisation.

By relating these problems and the solutions to which they gave rise to the economic circumstances which brought them about we are moving into the second area of investigation. This is the nature of poverty itself. The accounts are a record of the response to poverty, not of poverty itself, but they are the starting point for any investigation of the problems whose solutions they record. Essentially they provide three items of information: the names of the poor, what kind of relief they received (pension, rent, medical, workhouse, etc), and how long it lasted. What they hardly ever do is indicate why relief was granted. This must be deduced both directly from the information in the accounts and indirectly by linking this with information from other sources. For example, parish registers can be used to identify cases where old age, widowhood, or an exceptionally large family may have been significant factors in making a particular individual resort to public assistance. Similarly a broad knowledge of the economy both locally, in terms of the rise and fall of particular industries or enterprises, and nationally, in terms of the relationship between weather and harvest or the cycle of booms and slumps, can provide the context in which relief granted to those in the prime of life with no obvious reason for needing it may be understood.

Finally, the accounts can be used to reconstruct a detailed picture of the lives and life experiences of individual people. Because of the way the accounts were compiled we can piece together quite full stories about individuals who were supported by the parish over a prolonged period of time. Indeed, this information is so voluminous that from the late seventeenth to the early nineteenth centuries the very lowest section of the community, those in receipt of parish relief, is one of the best documented. Certainly we can learn more of their homes, their clothing, their bedding, their fuel, their health and their lives generally than we can about those immediately above them who kept no records of their activities and are often no more than names to the historian. On a broader level one might also generalise from the standard of living provided for the poor, as it is documented in these accounts, to form some impression of the minimum levels acceptable generally at any particular time.

At first sight overseers' accounts can appear daunting. Entry follows entry in an almost interminable progression of apparently inconsequential minutiae. Yet it is the sheer quantity of information that makes these records so valuable. From the mass of detail we can distil a general picture in which broad themes and trends can be identified and the typical is clearly distinguished from the unusual. Indeed, the many opportunities which they offer for tracing the stages by which a form of poverty or a method of relief evolved from the latter to the former is one of the characteristics which makes overseers' accounts such a fruitful source.

LOCATION

Overseers' accounts will usually be found in local record offices among the other records of civil parish administration.

BIBLIOGRAPHY

Hampson M, *The Treatment of Poverty in Cambridgeshire,* (Cambridge, 1934)

Marshall J D, *The Old Poor Law* (1968)

Oxley G W, *Poor Relief in England and Wales, 1601-1834* (Newton Abbot, 1974)

Slack P, *English Poor Law, 1531-1750* (1990)

Slack P, *Poverty and Policy in Tudor and Stuart England* (1988)

28

Settlement Papers

Kathryn M Thompson

[Settlement Examination of Mary Saunders, 1740]

This Examinant sayeth on Oath that she was married to Peter Saunders, shoemaker, ab[ou]t nine years ago at the Fleet in a house known by the Sign of the Hand & Pen, at Fleet Ditch; that she has been told by her husband that he was born & did belong to Cork in Ireland; that her maiden name was Mary Allen & that, as she has been informed, she was born at Ratcliff-bridge in the County of Lancaster ab[ou]t 4 miles from Manchester; that since her birth she has obtained sev[era]l settlem[en]ts by service the last of w[hi]ch was at Waterpenny in the County of Oxford, where she was hired by the year by one Mr Brown a farmer for four pounds for the year, w[hi]ch said service she fully performed; & that she has never gained any settlement since; that she had now three children by the said Peter Saunders now living, the Eldest, named Thomas born in Holborn over ag[ain]st the Vine Tavern, the Second, Elizabeth born at Hampstead in Middlesex, the Third, not yet baptised, born at Royston in Hertfordshire. That her husband dyed ab[ou]t half a year ago & was buried at St Andrews Holborn & further sayeth not.

Hertfordshire Record Office, Royston parish records, D/P 87 13/3/3

BACKGROUND

Although the principle of settlement was not specifically mentioned in the great poor law legislation of 1597 to 1601, parishes had been familiar with the problem for some time. They usually relied on the 1589 'Act Against Erecting and Maintaining Cottages' whose purpose was to reduce rural poverty by preventing over-population of villages where the opportunities for employment were restricted by the availability of land. No cottages were to be erected unless four acres of land were put with them and the keeping of lodgers was prohibited.

The idea that everyone had a place of settlement to which he or she could be returned in case of need was implicit in the laws against vagrancy and in the activities of overseers against 'strangers'. However it was not until the Act of Settlement of 1662 that previous assumptions and practices were codified and applied directly to the problems of poor relief. The central provision of the Act authorised two justices of the peace to remove any newcomers who were 'likely to be chargeable' to a parish, provided that complaint was made against them within 40 days of arrival and that they had not rented houses worth £10 or more a year or found security to discharge the parish from all expenses. As an afterthought a clause was added permitting continued residence in certain circumstances if migrants brought a certificate from their home parish acknowledging responsibility for them. Forty days' residence remained the basic qualification for gaining a settlement.

In 1691 the Act of Settlement was made permanent and additional ways of gaining a settlement introduced: in addition to birth a settlement could be gained by serving a parish office, paying the parish rate, being bound apprentice to a parishioner or (if single) serving a year in service. Women took their husband's settlement on marriage. From 1 May 1697 poor persons could enter any parish if they had a settlement certificate and could only be removed after they became chargeable; this was an attempt to remove the bar to those seeking work outside their parish as a result of the 1662 Act. The settlement certificate, to be valid, had to be issued by the overseers of the poor and the churchwardens, attested by two witnesses and approved by two magistrates. In practice, only the better off who could rent a £10 tenement, pay taxes or serve an office, or the young — over whose servitude or apprenticeship the parish had no control — could change their settlement easily.

Settlement was further refined during the life of the old poor law. It was not abolished by the 1834 Poor Law Amendment Act which made the union the unit of poor law administration, although certain ways of gaining a settlement (such as by hiring and service for a year or by serving a parish office) were abolished. It remained on a parochial basis, so that parishes in the same union became involved in lengthy and expensive legal battles. There were a number of other problems but attempts to solve them failed and the Settlement Acts remained, amended but unrepealed, until 1948.

Endless time and vast amounts of public money were spent on contested settlement cases. As much as half the business at quarter sessions could consist of deciding appeals against removal; the cost would often have covered the expense of a pauper's maintenance several times over. Under the new poor law the surviving correspondence of a Union clerk shows how much time and effort was devoted to settlement and removal. Removal was often suspended because of illness or other incapacity, and in many cases was never actually carried out.

The main documents generated by the settlement system were settlement certificates, removal orders and settlement examinations but others included appeals, counsel's opinions, vagrant examinations and passes, and records relating to pauper apprenticeship and to bastardy. (These last are the subject of *Guide* no 29.) Vestry minutes record the appointment of overseers of the poor and may contain other information about the poor law system in the parish concerned, but there is no general pattern and the amount of detail varies considerably.

USES OF THE RECORDS

Records of poor relief are one of the few sources for our knowledge and understanding of the lives of those at the lower end of the social spectrum but their uneven survival is frustrating. They can, if they exist in sufficient quantity and quality, give an excellent picture of the amount and types of poverty and of the lives of the working classes, when they fell below the poverty line. They also show the amount and type of migration, often demonstrating the extent of mobility in an age of poor communications. Settlement examinations are particularly informative, providing as they do a 'potted biography' of an individual; the document shown above is a good example of the complex settlement pattern to be found in one 'ordinary' family and helps to dispel the myth that people did not move far from their birthplace before the advent of railways.

The records are of course also of great interest to family historians. The existence of settlement papers, particularly where a number of inter-related documents are available, can provide an unrivalled source, putting the flesh on the bones of an otherwise one-dimensional ancestor, or providing a vital clue to an elusive member of the family.

The stream of questions posed by the records demonstrates their significance to a far wider field of social history than poor relief alone: examples include housing conditions, the treatment of illness, death and burial, and working practices.

FORMAT AND LOCATION

The records found with other parish material are single paper documents although in some parishes they were entered into a book, variously called a town book, parish book or similar. The documents are totally hand-written at first but by the 1740s printed forms were in use for the major types, requiring only the relevant information to be inserted. They vary in the amount of information they provide: a settlement certificate may just give the owner as 'John Smith and family' or may give precise names and ages of all the family members.

There are very few records between 1640 and 1700: few of the early temporary settlement certificates survive but from 1697 to 1795 there are hundreds, if not thousands, in every local authority record office. From 1795 the quantity of paper connected with removal increased and removal orders form the second largest category of records, after settlement certificates.

There are two main locations: with other parish records and in quarter sessions records. Although the administration of poor relief was a 'civil' function the records were almost always kept in the parish chest with the ecclesiastical material. Where the parish records have been deposited in a local authority record office they invariably include the settlement (and other poor law) records, but occasionally they are more properly kept with the records of the parish council. Some records therefore may still be with the parish or, in exceptional circumstances, may be in private hands, but the local county record office should be aware of their existence.

The records of the court of quarter sessions will almost always be found in the relevant county or city record office. The earliest ones date from the sixteenth century but in some counties may start a century later or, in a very few cases, not survive at all. The court of quarter sessions was the court of appeal from the decisions of the overseers of the poor. It also raised and administered funds for pensions for maimed soldiers (Acts of 1592-3 and 1601); the relief of prisoners in the King's Bench and Marshalsea prisons (Act of 1601); and poor prisoners in county gaols (Act of 1572). The records may include orders concerning settlement and removal, appeals against orders, against the action of the overseers or against poor rate assessments, as well as inter-parish disputes. After 1662 they also include appeals against removal orders.

ANCILLARY RECORDS

Settlement papers are just a part of a much wider group of records. The prime source for the history of poor relief in a parish is the overseers of the poor accounts (see *Guide* no 27) but there are any number of others. Details of the types of records which might survive can be found in Tate, *The Parish Chest* and the existence of records after 1834 is detailed in the Gibson guide, *Poor Law Union records* (4 volumes, 1993). Several record offices have written guides to the poor law records in their care.

Legal texts contain a mass of reports relating to settlement and removal and there were several printed guides for officers, especially in the nineteenth century. Town or borough records frequently include poor law material, such as bonds for the security of parishes authorised by the 1662 Act of Settlement, and the quarter sessions rolls are another fruitful source, as already indicated.

BIBLIOGRAPHY

Gibson, J, *Poor Law Union Records* (4 volumes, 1993)

Oxley, G W, *Poor Relief in England and Wales 1601-1834* (Newton Abbot, 1974)

Rose, M E, *The English Poor Law 1780-1930* (Newton Abbot, 1971)

Slack, P, *Poverty and Policy in Tudor & Stuart England* (1988)

Snell, K D M, *Annals of the Labouring Poor* (Cambridge, 1985)

Tate, W E, *The Parish Chest* (Chichester, 1983)

Taylor, J S, 'The Impact of Pauper Settlement 1691-1834', *Past and Present,* 73 (1976)

Webb, S & B, *English Poor Law History, Part I: The Old Poor Law* (1929, reprinted 1963)

Apprenticeship and Bastardy Records

Kathryn M Thompson

[Terms for taking apprentices by the Holywell Twist Company [c 1800]]

Children to be four feet 2 Inches high — to have two Compleat suits of Cloathes, or one suit and two Guineas — to be bound till 21 Years of age — and deliver'd to the Company's Agent in London — when out of their time they will recieve two new suits of Cloathes — Girls may then earn from five to 7s per week, Boys from 10 to 15s or more according to their ability — on Sundays they are taught to read at the expence of the Company.
Hertfordshire Record Office, Royston parish records, D/P 87 14/1/6

[Bastardy Examination of Elisabeth Dalkin of Royston, 1769]

This deponent saith on oath that she was delivered of a Male Child on [sic] October 1768 & Baptized by the Name of John & that she was never married, & the said Child was born of her Body in the Town of Royston aforesaid & on her oath she the said Elisabeth Dalkin declares before me Ralph Freman one of his Majesties Justices of the Peace for this County before whom she is brought that Joseph Finch the younger of the Parish of Benet in the Town of Cambridge is the Father of the said Child.
Hertfordshire Record Office, Royston parish records, D/P 87 15/1/29

BACKGROUND AND ORIGIN

Children who could not be cared for as part of a family presented a problem to poor law administrators, as they frequently lacked any means of support and were too young to earn their own living. The poor law Act of 1597 (39 Eliz, c 3) empowered overseers of the poor and churchwardens to set to work children whose parents were not considered able to keep them: the system of parish apprenticeship continued throughout the life of the old poor law and into the twentieth century, although compulsory apprenticeship was abolished in 1844. Illegitimate children presented another problem and successive acts of parliament attempted to solve it; the mothers and putative fathers of bastard children were pursued, both to punish them and to recoup the costs of providing for such children.

Apprenticeship was carried out by voluntary consent and by the parish officers; both forms gave the apprentice a settlement after 40 days' service. In addition to the system of pauper apprenticeship there were also private charities which made provision for apprenticing poor children. When a parish wanted to bind a poor child within its limits the chosen master had to take the boy or girl: in some parishes fines for excusal provided a regular and substantial income. Apprenticeship was sometimes done by rotation or drawn for in a kind of raffle, with the 'winners' drawing blanks. By the eighteenth century the old rules regarding apprenticeship were disappearing and it could be a fiction to dispose of a pauper child, often in someone else's parish. Children were apprenticed to the rather dubious 'trades' of husbandry or housewifery.

Under these circumstances there was considerable scope for ill-treatment; provision was made to protect apprentices in Acts of 1746-7, 1792 and 1792-3, including a system for checking on children sent to distant factories. Evidence of ill-usage is not as common as might be expected but, considering how difficult it was for an apprentice to draw attention to ill-treatment — let alone to get redress — it was almost certainly more prevalent than the records indicate. An Act of 1765-6 which authorised the apprehension and imprisonment of runaway apprentices, suggests a significant problem.

In the second half of the eighteenth century a considerable number of pauper children were sent to textile mills in the midlands and north. Factory owners used recruiting agents to find parents willing to send their children, and agents in the north asked overseers of the poor to provide children; London, not surprisingly, supplied the most children. In some cases parishes themselves offered recruits. The Health and Morals of Apprentices Act of 1802 was a major landmark in regulating the use of parish children in cotton mills and other factories, but in fact was already redundant by the time it was enacted, as from the 1790s new cotton mills required less apprentices to operate the machinery. An Act of 1816 made it illegal to apprentice London children more than 40 miles from their parish.

The system of apprenticeship continued under the new poor law despite the attempts by the legislators to end it. Total abolition proved impossible but legislation in 1844 and 1851 was designed to restrict the terms of apprenticeship and thus avoid the worst abuses.

In the sixteenth and seventeenth centuries the birth of an illegitimate child in the average country parish seems to have been an unusual event but from about 1750 was so common as to cause little surprise. There has been considerable debate about the reasons for its growth: suggestions have included the increased difficulty of getting accommodation and of leaving the parish of settlement; labourers were compelled to live where they could, often in overcrowded conditions, and the old moral restraints had gone.

Parish officers tried to compel marriage when an unmarried woman became pregnant — so-called 'knobstick' weddings — as a child born more than a month after the marriage was legitimate. A legitimate child usually took its father's settlement whereas an illegitimate one had a settlement in the place where the birth occurred; however bastard children of vagrant women were excluded from this provision. Under an Act of 1609-10 any 'lewd' woman with a chargeable bastard could be sent to a House of Correction for a year and if she offended again was to be sent back until she gave securities for good behaviour; this encouraged abortion and infanticide.

Under the 1662 Act of Settlement, if the parents of a bastard child absconded, the overseers of the poor could seize their goods. It appears that women kept quiet about their condition, hoping to dispose of the child quietly, and the fathers often disputed paternity. An Act of 1732-3 forced women pregnant with a bastard child to declare the fact and name the father; a man charged on oath with being the father of a bastard child was to be apprehended and committed to gaol unless he gave a security to indemnify the parish. A further Act of 1743-4 stated that a bastard born in a place where the mother was not settled was to take its mother's settlement.

Until about 1750 it seems that the parish officers dealt with the problem without much fuss. The vast majority of bastard births merely have an entry in the baptism register. There is evidence of sympathy from overseers of the poor and few cases were brought to quarter sessions. Problems not surprisingly increased as the incidence of illegitimacy grew. However the bulk of bastardy records tend to give the impression that a far greater proportion of overseers' time and money was spent on these matters than was the case.

USES OF THE RECORDS

Apprenticeship indentures are the principal records for a study of the subject. They survive in very great numbers, usually only exceeded by settlement certificates and removal orders (see *Guide* no 28) and the quantity of documents give it more significance than it actually had. Other records include accounts and bonds; the bonds can be copied in parish registers, overseers' accounts or vestry minutes. Apprenticeship by agreement may be recorded in parish registers or vestry minutes and the latter may also include agreements for clothing apprentices. Under an Act of 1801-2 an apprenticeship register was to be kept, although these do not survive as often as historians would like. Sending children to distant factories caused the creation of special documents, such as correspondence and agreements with factory owners.

The most obvious use of apprenticeship records is to provide information on local trades. Information on the popularity of different occupations, the age at which children began working and the distance they travelled to be apprenticed can all be discovered; this is considerably easier where an apprentice register survives. Indentures are increasingly being used for data input by local and family historians, often in conjunction with other poor law records. Pauper apprenticeship records can incidentally point to the attitude of local officials in economic affairs and can of course provide information generally on the incidence of poverty and the means employed to deal with it. However it is important to recognise that those records that survive may distort the overall picture.

Bastardy records include bonds, affiliation orders, examinations and warrants for the arrest of putative fathers. In addition baptism registers usually state if a child is illegitimate, even if no other records exist. Bastardy records in parish collections vary enormously in the rate of survival but where they do exist they give excellent data on the incidence of illegitimacy and the manner in which it was treated. The records, like all poor law material, are of great interest to family historians and the combination of bastardy records with other documents, such as apprenticeship indentures and settlement papers, can give a detailed account of an individual's circumstances.

FORMAT AND LOCATION

Like settlement and removal papers (see *Guide* no 28) apprenticeship and bastardy records are usually in the form of paper documents, latterly on pre-printed forms. They can also be entered in a book, known variously as a town book, parish book, or similar. Apprenticeship registers vary in size but most record the name of the apprentice, his or her parents (if alive), his or her age, the term of the apprenticeship and the name and occupation of the master.

These records will generally be found with the ecclesiastical parish material, having been kept together in the parish chest. Most of them are now deposited in local authority record offices, although some may still be in parish hands. As well as printed guides to poor law records in general many county record offices now have a personal names index to apprenticeship and bastardy records.

The records of the court of quarter sessions contain a lot of material relating to poor relief, such as orders for the maintenance of bastard children. In 1839 responsibility for pursuing putative fathers was transferred to petty sessions and after 1844 the clerks of the various divisions were required to make an annual return of all summons and orders concerning the maintenance of bastard children, and copies were sent to the Secretary of State.

Non-pauper apprenticeship records survive in town and borough records and those of charities which provided for the apprenticeship of poor children. These too will generally be found the county or city record office or sometimes in private hands. Solicitors whose practices have been established for several generations may well have such material in their files although the record office will normally be aware of it.

ANCILLARY RECORDS

Apprenticeship and bastardy records are only part of a much wider range of poor law material; further information on other sources will be found in *Guides* 27 and 28.

BIBLIOGRAPHY

Gibson, J, *Poor Law Union Records* (4 volumes, 1993)

Oxley, G W, *Poor Relief in England and Wales 1601-1834* (Newton Abbot, 1974)

Rose, M E, *The English Poor Law 1780-1930* (Newton Abbot, 1971)

Slack, P, *Poverty and Policy in Tudor & Stuart England* (1988)

Snell, K D M, *Annals of the Labouring Poor* (Cambridge, 1985)

Tate, W E, *The Parish Chest* (Chichester, 1983)

Thompson, K M, 'Apprenticeship and the New Poor Law: a Leicester example', *The Local Historian*, vol 19, no 2, May 1989

Webb, S & B, *English Poor Law History, Part I: The Old Poor Law* (1929, reprinted 1963)

30
Parish Registers
Christopher J Pickford

[Parish register of Willington, Beds, 1732 (BRO ref: P 26/1/1)]

1732

March ye 28 was buried Hannah Wells Wife of Edward Wells Labourer

April ye 10 was married Tho: Wilson & Mary Holloman both belonging to ye Parish of Cople by Bans

April ye 16 was Bap Elizabeth Pearch Daught^r of Richard Pearch & Elizabeth his Wife

May ye 8th was Bap: Ann Newil Daughter of John Newil Blacksmith & Ann His Wife

May ye 28th: was marry'd Thomas Bell of Eaton Socon & Judith Negus of St Neots by Licence

June ye 5th was buried Ann Newil an Infant Daughter of John Newil Blacksmith & Ann his Wife

July ye 23 was Bap: William Son of Thomas and Mary Abrahams

July ye 27 was Buried Ann Newil Wife of John Newil Blacksmith

Sep: 10th was Baptiz'd Susanna Yates Daughter of Ann & Joseph Yates Labourer

October ye Ist was buried Isaac Titford Son of William & Mary Titford

Nov: 7th was buried Seth Garret Carpenter

Nov: 8: was buried Henry Childs Son of Matthew Childs Ale Keeper & Mary his Wife

[n.b. 'ye' should be read as 'the'; what appears to be a 'y' is in fact an Anglo Saxon letter (thorn), representing 'th']

ORIGIN AND BACKGROUND

Nowadays we take the registration of births, marriages and deaths for granted and assume that proof of these events can be obtained when needed. This is not altogether surprising, since the system in use today has evolved over four and a half centuries, beginning with the introduction of parish registers in the reign of King Henry VIII.

A few parishes are fortunate enough to possess registers dating from 1538 when the systematic recording of all baptisms, marriages and burials in church was first required by law. These early registers were often kept on paper. More often, the earliest surviving register will date from 1558 — the beginning of the reign of Queen Elizabeth I — in compliance with an injunction of 1599 which required the use of parchment instead of paper and called for the earliest registers to be copied out afresh on parchment. This explains why the entries for the sixty years up to 1600 often appear to have all been written at the same time and in the same hand.

Parish Registers

During the Commonwealth period the system of registration was sometimes neglected and the surviving registers are consequently defective. However, this period also saw a brave experiment in civil registration in the recording of births (instead of baptisms) and civil marriages. In 1653, each parish was required to elect a registrar — confusingly called a parish register — to record these events. This was abruptly curtailed at the Restoration of the Monarchy in 1660 when the use of registers of baptisms, marriages and burials resumed.

In 1666 legislation was introduced to give support to the declining woollen industry. The use of woollen shrouds for burials became compulsory, and fines — contemptuously regarded as fees by the wealthier classes — were introduced as a penalty for burials in finer materials. Special registers containing certificates of burial in woollen began in this period, but often fell into disuse before the laws were finally repealed in 1814.

The first attempt to standardise register format came in 1754 under Lord Hardwicke's marriage act which introduced standard forms for marriage entries and required the publication of banns to be formally recorded. Parties were required to sign the register — or make their mark — and the signatures of witnesses became necessary. The act was intended to solve the problem of fraudulent marriages by tightening up on procedures.

In the 1770s, Shute Barrington (1734-1826) — successively bishop of Llandaff, Salisbury and Durham — became concerned about the standard of record-keeping in parish registers. In association with the historian John Nichols and others, he produced new printed register books for baptisms and burials. Published in 1781 these were sold commercially, and used surprisingly widely in various parts of the country. These record details often not found in ordinary registers. The burial register, for instance, records age, cause of death, and position of interment.

Under Rose's act of 1812, the format for all registers was standardised. Separate printed books were introduced for baptisms, marriages and burials — each requiring the clergyman or clerk to record specific information in every entry. The marriage register, although redesigned, was little altered, but the registers for baptisms and burials underwent significant change. For the first time, baptism registers from 1813 record an address (place of abode) for the family and state the father's trade or occupation. Burial registers also give an address, together with the age of the deceased. A new form of register for banns of marriage came into use in 1823.

Parish registers have continued since the introduction of civil registration in 1837, the post-1837 church marriage registers doubling up as the civil record. Additionally from this time, the marriage registers give the age and occupation of the bride and groom, and their respective fathers' names and occupations.

To some extent, registers of baptisms and burials were superseded by the new civil registers of births and deaths yet they have continued to be kept for ecclesiastical purposes. For the user, the church records have the advantage that, unlike the civil registration records, they are available for study. Modern parish records will also contain registers of confirmations, registers of church services, and records of funerals and interments of ashes.

It is important to remember that parish registers, whatever else they may contain, are the creation and inheritance of the established church. They are not comprehensive records of registration, and users must always be aware of their limitations in this respect. Members of the nonconformist churches, especially, will be omitted.

USES

Commonly recognised as a principal source of information for family historians, parish registers have been somewhat neglected by students of other disciplines. One notable exception is the work of the Cambridge Population Studies Group whose statistical analysis of parish register entries has led to exciting discoveries about the past and to the radical re-appraisal of traditional theories. Their journal *Local Population Studies* contains the results of research into demographic trends based on parish registers and ancillary sources.

Parish registers enable the historian to identify individual members of society and piece together biographical information on key people involved in historical events. These details may be the stuff of footnotes rather than mainstream text, but they are no less vital to a genuine understanding of the past.

At the most simple level, registers can be used to trace information on the place and date of birth, marriage and death of people. Family groupings can be established, and relationships between individuals and families can also be discovered. Modern aids, such as published transcripts and indexes, and the International Genealogical Index (IGI) have made such searches far easier today than they were even ten years ago.

Where the register entries contain more than just the baldest of detail, then all sorts of other uses become possible. Even before 1812, the father's trade or occupation may be given in baptismal entries making it possible to study the socio-economic composition of a town parish or village. Levels of literacy of couples getting married can be studied from post-1754 marriage registers, linked perhaps to the availability of educational opportunities in different villages. Causes of death and ages given in burial entries similarly provide ample scope for analysis and contextual evaluation.

By combing through the registers for unusual entries, the historian can often find clues for further research. The establishment of local newspapers in the eighteenth century created a demand for interesting news, and happenings such as the births of deformed infants, and accidental deaths found ready press coverage. Wry comments alongside entries can also give useful insight to contemporary perceptions and values. When three base-born children were baptised at Houghton Regis (Beds.) on 13 September 1761 the Rector noted 'A very memorable thing three bastards christened the same time', but alongside someone added in a later hand 'Not so remarkable for Bedfordshire'.

LOCATION — ORIGINAL REGISTERS AND COPIES

Under current ecclesiastical legislation, it is now a requirement for parish registers, except for the most recent, to be deposited in a designated Diocesan

Record Office (usually the same as the County Record Office for the area) . Only if strict conditions are met may records be retained in parochial custody. As a result, parish registers are more likely to be held at the Record Office than at the church. Users wishing to see them will be best advised initially to contact the County or Diocesan archivist who will know where the records of a given parish for a specified date are held.

Many parish registers have been transcribed, indexed and published, making access easier for the user. The marriage entries for a great many parishes have been published in the Phillimore series, county publication schemes such as that in Bedfordshire have seen many early registers into print, and the registers of numerous parishes have been privately published.

Through the work of the Genealogical Society of Utah (GSU), which has been microfilming parish registers and other genealogical sources for many years, microfilm copies of many original registers have been made accessible throughout the world, especially in GSU Family History Centres. Local microfilming programmes have also helped to make register copies more widely available, for instance in branch libraries.

The IGI, a county-by-county alphabetical name index of baptism and marriage entries, is an invaluable research aid compiled as a by-product of the GSU microfilming programme. Excellent as it is, the IGI should never be used as a source. It is only an index, and all information found in it should be checked in the original registers or in a reliable transcript.

FORMAT AND CONTENTS

Original registers take different forms at various periods, depending on the format prescribed by law. The earliest registers are often 'free-text' (to use a term from modern computer jargon) containing mixed entries of baptisms, marriages and burials and with wide variation in the amount of information given in each entry. Register entries before 1754 (for marriages) and 1813 (baptisms and burials) are often of mixed type, and not always in chronological order. Some indications of the changes in format from the sixteenth century to modern times are given above, being inextricably linked to the statutory framework under which registers were compiled.

The nature of the parish register as an enduring record made it suitable for recording other important events and information for posterity. Parish register memoranda can be immensely useful to the local historian, including such topics as the beating of the bounds, gifts to the church, floods and tempests, lists of inhabitants, remedies for rabies — 'to cure the bite of a mad Dog' — and the like. They are, however, difficult to find. Ideally Record Offices should list memoranda in their catalogues and make sure that they are adequately indexed. Similarly, all memoranda should be included in published editions of registers.

ANCILLARY RECORDS

Apart from the modern aids to the use of registers mentioned above, the principal ancillary sources are the Bishops Transcripts — contemporary copies of the

register entries that were required to be submitted annually to the diocesan registry under an order made in 1597. For most dioceses, files of register transcripts survive — in varying degrees of completeness — from around 1600 to the late nineteenth century. These can be used to fill gaps in the surviving registers for a given parish, and to validate — and in some cases provide additional information — documented baptisms, marriages and burials. Poor law bastardy papers, and the records of disputed cases in Petty and Quarter Sessions records, can be useful in establishing the parentage of illegitimate infants for whom only one parent is named in the baptism register.

Marriage entries may be supported by registers of banns (at least from 1754) and by marriage licences, bonds and allegations. The latter, often dating from as far back as the early seventeenth century, will be found among Diocesan and Archidiaconal archives and may give useful additional information on the parties to a marriage. Banns were publicly called three times prior to marriage and recorded in the registers of the bride and groom's parishes.

Although they only deal with a fairly small proportion of the population, probate records — wills, administrations and probate inventories — can profitably be used alongside burial records to provide information on the circumstances of individuals at the time of their death.

From the eighteenth century, the nonconformist churches began to keep their own registers of births (or baptisms) and deaths (or burials), as dissenters found themselves disadvantaged by being unable to prove their identity. These registers were chiefly surrendered to the Registrar General in 1837, and are now at the Public Record Office (class RG 4). Microfilm copies are generally available locally, along with some original registers retained by the churches. These records can be used alongside parish registers to provide information omitted from the registers and to give a fuller picture of the composition of local communities.

BIBLIOGRAPHY

Cox, J C, *The Parish Registers of England* (1910)

Gibson, Jeremy, *Bishops' Transcripts and Marriage Licences, Bonds and Allegations: a Guide to their Location and Indexes* (Federation of Family History Societies, 3rd ed, 1991)

National index of Parish Registers (Society of Genealogists) Vol 1 general introduction, and Vols 4-13 area guides

Tate, W E, *The Parish Chest* (3rd ed, Cambridge, 1969) — chapter on 'Parish Registers', pp.43-83.

Archdeacons' Records

C. C. Webb and David M. Smith

ORIGIN AND DEVELOPMENT OF THE OFFICE

Hamilton Thompson traced the origin of the office of archdeacon to the early Christian church, but the structure of diocesan organisation in the English Church, including the growth and development of territorial archdeaconries, developed in the period after the Norman conquest and persisted throughout the middle ages and beyond. The structure, however, was never uniform. Some dioceses (eg Canterbury, Rochester, Ely and Carlisle) had only one archdeaconry. In contrast, large dioceses developed archdeaconries based on regional subdivisions; Lincoln had eight archdeaconries from the twelfth century and in the northern province York had five archdeaconries in the middle ages.

FUNCTIONS OF THE OFFICE

On the Continent there was at times, particularly in the twelfth and thirteenth centuries, rivalry between the authority of the archdeacon and that of his bishop. This does not seem ever to have been a problem in England, where the characteristic function of the archdeacon was to assist his diocesan bishop in the administration of his see, and for this reason was often called the *oculus episcopi* (the bishop's eye). Nevertheless, the prestige of the office in the medieval period was great, if we are to judge by the imposing progresses made by some archdeacons, accompanied by many servants and carriages, sometimes equalling in pomp the progress of a bishop. On the other hand, this outward show of authority and status was balanced by some opinion that archdeacons had little chance of salvation, being much addicted to the taking of bribes, and rejoicing in false accusations. As with other offices, some archdeacons fulfilled their duties by means of a deputy; others, however, were assiduous in the performance of their duties.

The archdeacon was dependent upon the mandate of his bishop, and executed the bishop's day-to-day orders in such tasks as the induction of new incumbents to their livings, and the general oversight of churches, clergy and laity within his archdeaconry. In the course of time, most archdeacons acquired rights of visitation (which were inhibited during an episcopal visitation) and correction. The archdeacon might also hold a probate court, especially when the usual episcopal consistory court was difficult of access. In some cases, where archdeaconries were geographically isolated from the centre of diocesan administration (as with the case of the archdeaconries of Nottingham and Richmond in the medieval diocese of York) their archdeacons developed additional jurisdictional rights and responsibilities. By the sixteenth century, these two archdeaconries were virtually autonomous jurisdictions, (although of course they were still reliant on the archbishop for specifically episcopal functions, such as ordination). The archdeaconry of Nottingham had a consistory and correction court and an administration that was entirely distinct from that of the archbishop; the archdeacon of Richmond possessed the powers of admission and institution of clergy to benefices within his archdeaconry.

The extent to which the powers of the archdeacon were brought to bear varied considerably with the personality of the individual who held the office, and with the changing nature of the Church; the ebb and flow of post-Reformation changes can be observed in the detail of the court records in particular. After the Toleration Act of 1689 the nature of the business conducted in the archidiaconal courts changed, being confined principally to moral offences and to regulating the state of the fabric of churches. As with episcopal visitations, the aim of the archdeacons gradually moved away from simple detection and correction and towards the gathering of information, mainly about the state of the Church and the strength and nature of nonconformity.

By the nineteenth century, if not before, archidiacional visitations had come to collect information about the state of the fabric of the church and associated buildings such as the parsonage, the number and nature of regular services, the clergy working in each parish, educational provision and the nature and strength of dissenting congregations. The information so gathered was used to issue orders for the improvement of any defects discovered, and the findings of previous visitations were often referred to on subsequent visits.

RECORDS OF ARCHDEACONS

The archdeacon's annual visitations to keep an eye on the spiritual and moral welfare of his flock, both ecclesiastical and lay, and the work of his court, produced voluminous visitation and court books, (which can sometimes be more in the nature of general act books, containing induction mandates, citation mandates, inhibitions, relaxations and the like, rather than simply court books). Files supplementing the main visitation and court records can include returns to articles of enquiry, presentments, correction citations, excommunications, penances and churchwardens' oaths and declarations. The archdeacon's need to keep a check on the physical fabric of the churches in his archdeaconry sometimes caused him to make special records of the state of church fabric and of orders for remedying any defects he discovered. In addition, files of miscellaneous correspondence illustrating the whole range of archidiaconal responsibilities and duties have survived for a few archdeaconries. In some places there are papers, (which might include citations, calls and poll lists) relating to the election of Convocation proctors for an archdeaconry. Records of the payment of fees, principally the collection of procurations for episcopal and archidiaconal visitations, survive in some places as separate volumes, supplemented by files showing the extent of arrears; in other places similar information can be found in visitation call books.

LOCATION OF RECORDS

Many archidiaconal records are kept together with the relevant diocesan records in the designated diocesan record office, and are included in the published guides to these offices. For location of the records of archdeacons' testamentary jurisdictions a valuable guide is J.S.W. Gibson, *Wills and where to find them*, (Chichester, 1974).

BIBLIOGRAPHY

For the growth, development and powers of archdeacons a good account is **A. Hamilton-Thompson,** *Diocesan Organisation in the Middle Ages: Archdeacons and Rural Deans*, (Raleigh Lecture, British Academy, 1943, printed also in *Proceedings of the British Academy,* xxix (1943), pp. 153-194). More recent studies are **B. Kemp**, 'Archdeacons and Parish Churches in England in the Twelfth Century' in G. Garnett and J. Hudson (eds.), *Law and Government in Medieval England and Normandy: essays in honour of Sir James Holt*, (Cambridge, 1994), pp. 341-364; **B. Kemp**, 'Informing the Archdeacon on Ecclesiastical Matters in Twelfth-Century England' in M.J. Franklin and C. Harper-Bill (eds.), *Medieval Ecclesiastical Studies in Honour of Dorothy M. Owen*, Studies in the History of Medieval Religion 7, Woodbridge, 1995), pp. 131-149; **M. Burger**, 'Bishops, Archdeacons and communication between centre and locality in the diocese of Lincoln *c.* 1214-99', in P.R. Coss and S.D. Lloyd (eds.) *Thirteenth Century England V*, (Woodbridge, 1995), pp. 195-206; **J. Sayers**, 'Monastic Archdeacons' in C.N.L. Brooke, D.E. Luscombe, G.H. Martin and D. Owen (eds.) *Church and Government in the Middle Ages: essays presented to C.R. Cheney on his 70th birthday* (Cambridge, 1976), pp. 177-203; **E.M. Elvey**, 'Early Records of the Archdeaconry of Buckingham: their importance to the social historian', in *Records of Buckinghamshire*, 19 (1971), pp. 55-66; **M. Bowker**, 'Some Archdeacons' Court Books and the Commons' Supplication against the Ordinaries of 1532', in D.A. Bullough and R.L. Storey (eds.), *The Study of Medieval Records: Essays in Honour of Kathleen Major*, (Oxford, 1971). There is a detailed study of the archdeaconry of Nottingham in the early modern period in **R.A. Marchant**, *The Church Under the Law: justice, administration and discipline in the diocese of York 1560-1640*, (Cambridge, 1969), pp. 147-203.

Identifications of archdeaconries and their geographical areas can be found in **D.M. Smith**, *Guide to Bishops' Registers of England and Wales: a survey from the Middle Ages to the Abolition of Episcopacy in 1646*, (Royal Historical Society Guides and Handbooks 11, 1981) and in **F.A. Youngs**, *Guide to the Local Administrative Units of England I: Southern England and II: Northern England*, (Royal Historical Society Guides and Handbooks 10 and 17, 1981 and 1991).

Editions of records include for the medieval period **C.L. Feltoe and E.H. Minns** (eds.), *Vetus Liber Eliensis*, (Cambridge Antiquarian Society octavo publications, 48, 1917); **A. Hamilton Thompson** (ed.), 'The registers of the archdeaconry of Richmond, 1361-1442' in *Yorkshire Archaeological Journal*, 25 (1920), pp. 129-268, and the continuation by the same editor, 'The register of the archdeacons of Richmond, 1442-1477' in *Yorkshire Archaeological Journal*, 30 (1931), pp. 1-134 and *YAJ*, 32 (1936), pp. 111-145. There are several editions of court and visitation records, including **E.M. Elvey** (ed.), *The Courts of the Archdeaconry of Buckingham 1483-1523*, (Buckinghamshire Record Society, 19, 1975); **E.R. Brinkworth** (ed.), *The Archdeacon's Court: liber actorum 1584* vol I and vol II (Oxfordshire Record Society, 23-24, 1942 and 1946); **A.P. Moore** (ed.), 'Proceedings of the ecclesiastical courts in the archdeaconry of Leicester, 1516-1535', in *Associated Architectural Societies: Reports and Papers*, 28 (1905-06), pp. 117-220; **C. Jenkins** (ed.), 'Act Book of the Archdeacon of Taunton [1623-4]' in *Collectanea II*, (Somerset Record Society, 43, 1928), pp. 1-175; **A.C. Wood** (ed.), 'The Nottinghamshire Presentment Bills of 1587', in *A Miscellany of Nottinghamshire Records*, (Thoroton Society Record Series, 11, 1945), pp. 1-42; **M.R. Austin** (ed.), *The Church in Derbyshire in 1823-4: the* *parochial visitation of Rev Samuel Butler, Archdeacon of Derby in the Diocese of Lichfield and Coventry*, (Derbyshire Archaeological Society Record series, 5, 1972); D. Robinson (ed.), *Visitations of the Archdeaconry of Stafford 1829-1841*, (Staffordshire Record Society, 10, 1980). A good idea of the range of correspondence and business being received by an archdeacon from a diocesan bishop and others is provided in the calendar by H.R. Wilton Hall, *Records of the old Archdeaconry of St Alban's: a calendar of papers AD 1575 to AD 1637*, (St Alban's and Hertfordshire Architectural and Archaeological Society, 1908).

EXAMPLES OF RECORDS

1. Churchwardens' presentments (Borthwick Institute, YV/ChP 1678).

The presentments of Christopher Bell and William Metcalf, chappelwardens of the chappell of Sowerby for the year 1678.

Imprimis we present Peter Darley and Dorothy his wife and Anne Best: Papists.

Item we present Peter Dail: Quaker.

[Signed] Christo:[pher] Bell, William Metcalfe

Item we present Matthew Morley of Thirsk and Susan Bell of Sowerby for not giving an account of their marriage and for refusing to shew a certificate by whom, where or when they were married.

The presentments of Thomas Banks, curate.

Imprimis I present William Metcalff for not paying his dues to the <church> curate of Sowerby.

Item I present Susanna Bell, now wife to Matthew Morley, who was then with in the chappelry of Sowerby, for not observing the fast day appointed by the Kings proclamation, but using servile work in the time of divine service.

[Signed] Tho:[mas] Banks, curate.

2. Record of an entry in a visitation court book (Borthwick InstituteYV/CB 5 ff.225v and 226)

Kettlewell: Omnia bene *[all is well]*

Kirkby Malhamdale: Similiter *[similar]*

Kildwick: Contra Gulielmum Lambert de Gilgrange *[against William Lambert of Gilgrange]* for deludeing Silly people, &pretending to be a Fortune teller, & to discover things lost.

Waddington:Officium Domini contra Thomam Parker de Grindleton et Elizabetham uxorem eius pretensam *[Office of the judge against Thomas Parker of Grindleton and Elizabeth his pretended wife]* for sowing strife and discord in the neighbourhood and for being railers, lyars and slanderers and alsoe for not certifying their pretended marriage as alsoe for fornicacion before marriage.

14 Julij 1703. Comparuit coram Cancellarium in camera sua infra clausum etc dictus Parker quem Dominus decrevit absolucionem unde emanavit *[On 14 July 1703 the said Parker appeared before the Chancellor in his chamber within the (Minster) close etc, upon which the Judge decreed absolution, whereupon it was issued].*

3 Record of a fabric inspection (Borthwick Institute YV/Ret 2 p19)

Die Lunae duodecimo die mensis Junij Anno Domini 1721 Inter horas Nona et duodecima ante meridiem ejusdem diei coram venerabilibus viris Carolo Blake STP, archidiacono archidiaconatus Ebor' et Gulielmo Ward LLD, officiali in presentia mei *[On Monday the 12th day of the month of July 1721 between the hours of 9 and 12 in the morning of the same day, before the venerable men Charles Blake DD, archdeacon of York and William Ward LLD, Official, in the presence of me]*

St Olavi extra muros civitatis Ebor' Comparuerunt Thomas Mosley, clericus, curatus ibidem, Johannes Hall, Gulielmus Smart, Thomas Chapman et Johannes Jackson, guardiani ibidem (inspectione dictae ecclesiae habita) Domini decreverunt *[St Olave's without the walls of the City of York. There appeared Thomas Mosley, clerk, curate there, John Hall, William Smart, Thomas Chapman and John Jackson, churchwardens there (an inspection of the said church having been conducted) the Judges decreed]* that the whole body of the church in the walls, windows, roofe and floor be repaired, the churchyard wall and fence to be repaired by the persons to whom the same belongeth, a new hood for the minister, one other lock and key to be provided before Michaelmas next. That the whole chancell to be repaired in the walls, windows, roofe, timber and floor and to be new white washed. The certificate of the repairs of the church and chancell in Michaelmas 1722.

4 Correspondence (Borthwick Institute YV/Misc)

Kighley Iune 11
1705
Dear S[i]r
I have this day enquired of Dan: Craven what answer to return you, & he sais that he is satisfyed as to his own pew in the church & has accordingly entred his name in the Register.

And for his other information about a pew for the Duke of Devonshire, he hereby desires it may rest till he is informed further from some of the stewards.

As for his being presented by the churchwardens for nor paying his Sess for the Mills, he is not willing to yeild & pay it.

Robert Wright who was presented for neglect of coming to church has complyed & promises for the future to come, so that both these desire to have their names left out of the citation.

For John Ramsbottom he defies any authority, since he has taken the Oathes, & runs to a meeting house at Bingley, but tis no matter what one of his practice professes.

This is all at present from y[ou]r humble servant

M: Gale

Bishops' Registers
David Robinson

[Register of William Melton, Archbishop of York 1317-1340 [Borthwick Institute of Historical Research, York, reg 9]]

INSTITUTIO ECCLESIE DE SOUTH KILVYNGTON

Willelmus etc. dilecto filio Nicholao Darel, clerico, salutem, graciam et benedictionem. Ad presentationem nobilis viri domini Galfridi de Upsale, militis, te de cuius meritis et virtutibus sinceram in Domino fiduciam obtinemus, ad ecclesiam de Southkilvyngton, nostre diocesis, per resignationem Johannis de Aldeburgh, ultimi rectoris eiusdem, vacantem, caritatis intuitu admittimus et rectorem instituimus canonice in eadem. Vale. Dat' apud Cawode, 14 Kalendas Septembris, anno gracie millesimo trecentisimo vicesimo nono, et pontificatus nostri duidecimo.

INDUCTIO EIUSDEM

Memorandum quod eisdem die et loco scriptum fuit ... archidiacono Cliveland' vel eius officiali ad inducendum predictum Nicholaum vel procuratorem suum eius nomine in corporalem possessionem predicte ecclesie cum suis iuribus et pertinenciis universis.

INSTITUTION TO THE CHURCH OF SOUTH KILVINGTON

William etc, to our beloved son Nicholas Darel, clerk, greeting, grace and benediction. At the presentation of the noble sir Geoffrey de Upsale, knight, we, prompted by affection, admit you, of whose merits and virtues we have sincere trust in the Lord, to the church of South Kilvington, vacant by the resignation of John de Aldeburgh, last rector of the same, and we have canonically instituted you in the same. [Date.]

INDUCTION OF THE SAME

Memorandum that on the same day and place [a letter] was written to the archdeacon of Cleveland or his official to induct the aforesaid Nicholas, or his proxy in his name, into corporal possession of the aforesaid church with all its rights and appurtenances.

ORIGIN

Bishops' registers are the single most important series of records created by episcopal administration in the middle ages. They vary in form and content from diocese to diocese and in some dioceses from bishop to bishop but their central feature is the institution of clergy to benefices. They may also include ordination lists, licences and dispensations for clergy and laity, visitation records, royal writs and copies of any documents issued or received by the bishop and judged worthy of permanent preservation.

The earliest surviving registers are those of Hugh of Wells, bishop of Lincoln, 1209-35 (surviving rolls begin about 1214-15) and Walter de Grey, archbishop of York, 1215-55 (surviving rolls begin in 1225). There is evidence of the keeping of registers in all other English dioceses before the end of the thirteenth century. By then rolls had been largely supplanted by quires which were bound into one or more volumes at the end of an episcopate. Some registers cover more than one episcopate. Good series of medieval registers have survived for most dioceses although there have been notable losses, especially of thirteenth century and early fourteenth century registers. In most dioceses, systematic series of other records begin in the sixteenth century and from that period the registers decline in range of contents. This *Guide* covers only medieval registers.

USING THE REGISTERS

Bishops' registers are in Latin, except for copies of documents of royal or other secular origin which may be in French or, in the later middle ages, English. Institutions, ordination lists and many licences are in standard form but less common entries may require a reasonable command of medieval Latin. The registers are usually written in a clear hand but some are heavily abbreviated. Manuscript indexes, medieval or later, are often found.

The Canterbury and York Society has published bishops' registers since 1909 and many registers have been published by local record societies or independently. In these editions, institutions and other common form entries are calendared in English. Other entries may be transcribed in full with a summary headnote in English but in more recent editions most entries are calendared.

There were seventeen medieval dioceses in England and four in Wales. The registers will be found in the appropriate local record office, usually in the cathedral city. Surviving Welsh registers are in the National Library of Wales. A bishop's jurisdiction did not extend over the whole area of his diocese: 'peculiar' jurisdictions covered many ecclesiastical and some other estates, including the properties of the dean and chapter or prior and convent of the cathedral church itself. These areas from which the bishop was largely excluded may make fewer appearances in the registers, although in some cases the bishop might enter copies of documents, for example, visitation records, with the specific intention of recording the precedent.

Between the death of one bishop and the consecration of another there was a period of vacancy. Jurisdiction then passed to the archbishop although in some dioceses his rights were restricted. Archbishops also possessed the right of visitation of dioceses in their province: researchers for any diocese should not overlook the archbishop's registers. Frequently vacancy business transacted by vicars general is found in the register of the succeeding bishop.

The legal and social background to many of the entries in a register may be complex. The inexperienced researcher may easily be led into misunderstandings or hasty judgements. An attempt is made in the next section to explain some of the dangers in importing modern assumptions and a number of general works of ecclesiastical history are listed in the bibliography.

Registers may be used to obtain quantitative evidence — length of benefice-holding, numbers and titles of ordinands, the granting of licences — but care must be taken to establish whether registration appears to be complete.

CONTENTS

The register of Thomas Bek, bishop of Lincoln 1324-47, contains 456 folios bound in three volumes: institutions of clergy, arranged by archdeaconry, and ordinations of chantries; general memoranda, licences and dispensations for clergy, and commissions, including commissions to receive criminous clerks from prison; ordinations of clergy, royal writs and visitation injunctions. This is a good example of some of the range of material which may be found in a register.

INSTITUTIONS OF CLERGY

The patron was successor in title to the lord who had initially founded the church for his tenants. The founder would normally be a layman or an ecclesiastical corporation such as a religious house. Many laymen later transferred their patronage to a religious house. When a benefice fell vacant by the death or resignation of the incumbent the patron presented a clerk to the bishop who, if the candidate was legally qualified to hold the benefice, instituted him and issued a mandate, usually to the archdeacon, to induct him. The clerk thereafter possessed a permanent title to his benefice, from which he could be removed only by due process of ecclesiastical law. The registration of his institution was evidence of the incumbent's right to hold his benefice and, in the longer term, of the patron's right to his patronage. For the researcher these entries provide a succession of incumbents' names and, where the cause of the vacancy is given, we have evidence of the completeness or otherwise of the resulting list.

LICENCES FOR THE CLERGY

Many clergy were given benefices as a means of supporting them while they were employed as lawyers or administrators in the service of the king, bishop or a religious house and many others, as the literate class, provided a variety of similar services for their patrons. Kings' and bishops' clerks did not need a licence for non-residence in the service of their masters. Other beneficed clergy, if they were rectors, could seek licences for non-residence in the service of their patrons. A benefice might also be a means of support while studying at university, and under the constitution 'Cum ex eo' of Gregory X (1274, republished by Boniface VIII in 1298), beneficed clergy could be granted dispensations for up to seven years for this purpose.

ORDINATION LISTS AND LETTERS DIMISSORY

Most medieval clergy never obtained a benefice. Some served as parish chaplains assisting a resident incumbent or taking the place of a non-resident.

Others lived by saying masses as and when they were required. These men rarely appear in ecclesiastical records other than in ordination lists.

Bishops ordained men at the four embertides and sometimes at other seasons. For each ordination there will usually be separate lists of subdeacons, deacons and priests ordained. Sometimes acolytes, the minor order below that of subdeacon, and very occasionally men receiving the first tonsure, are also listed. The candidates were examined, and sometimes in early registers traces of this may be found in the lists. Each candidate must show his 'title', the assured income on the security of which he was ordained, and this is stated in the lists. Monks, canons and friars also appear in the lists when they are ordained, their names usually preceded by 'fr' for 'frater' (brother).

If a man wished to be ordained in a diocese other than his native one, he needed 'letters dimissory' from his own bishop. These are usually recorded in the ordination lists, and the grant of letters dimissory is also frequently included in the register of the bishop granting them.

ORDINATIONS OF VICARAGES

Religious houses frequently sought financial benefit from churches in their patronage. Sometimes they were able to take over the full revenues of the rector and serve the church by either a member of the house or a stipendiary chaplain. From the thirteenth century bishops increasingly insisted that the religious house take only about two-thirds of the benefice income and endow a vicarage with the other third. Like a rector, the vicar (vicarius = deputy) would be presented, instituted and inducted and would have freehold possession of his benefice. He could not normally be non-resident, and must also be in priest's or deacon's orders: in the latter case he was expected to be ordained priest at the subsequent ordination. The 'ordination' of a vicarage may include a detailed description of the glebe lands, tithes and other property and rights divided between the religious house and the vicar.

ORDINATIONS OF CHANTRIES

Medieval men and women commonly left sums of money for masses to be said for their souls after death. From the fourteenth century onwards, many of the richer ones left endowments for perpetual chantries, by which sufficient income was left for one or more clergy to say mass for their souls and the souls of others in perpetuity. These masses might be celebrated at an existing church altar, in a newly-built chapel in a church such as the chantry chapels still to be seen in many cathedrals, or in free-standing chapels such as the Lovekyn chapel at Kingston upon Thames.

The formal establishment and endowment ('ordination') of such chantries includes descriptions of the property with which the chantry was endowed and of the duties of the chaplains. Many of the chantry priests became the schoolmasters of their towns and villages and the origins and endowment of many local grammar schools, ostensibly Edward VI or Queen Elizabeth I foundations, are found in the return by the Crown of the property of chantries abolished at the Reformation.

VISITATIONS

Visitations are the subject of *Guide* no 8. Records of visitations of monasteries and nunneries are quite common and these may include detailed descriptions of lapses in standards of sexual morality, worship, mutual charity or financial administration. Some bishops' registers include citations to visitations of parish churches, but there is rarely any record of the faults discovered.

OTHER ENTRIES

It is difficult to summarise the range of entries which may be found in registers. Some relate to the whole diocese, some to particular places or individuals. Entries cover much more than narrowly ecclesiastical matters. Royal writs are commonly entered in registers of some dioceses, and papal decrees may be found. The responsibility of the church for education may be seen in the appointment of a grammar school master.

Social life may be illustrated by an injunction against sorcery or divination or against playing games in a churchyard, economic life by a dispute over tithes, religious belief by the prosecution of Lollard heretics. The bishop might issue to a suffragan bishop a commission to ordain or confirm, to reconcile a church or churchyard polluted by the shedding of blood, or to consecrate or dedicate churches, churchyards, altars and chapels. Wills are found in some registers, notably those of the archiepiscopal sees of Canterbury and York.

An indulgence for repairing a church may help to date architectural work. Laymen and women might be granted licences for private oratories or chapels, or dispensations to eat meat during Lent. There may be a detailed account of the election of a head of a religious house or the penance of a delinquent inmate. The bishop might issue a commission to his clerks to enquire into the status of a chapel, or the reason for two clergymen wishing to exchange their benefices, or into a matrimonial or tithe dispute. Researchers into most aspects of medieval history will find relevant material in bishops' registers.

BIBLIOGRAPHY

Churchill, I J, *Canterbury Administration* (2 vols, London, 1933)

Haines, R M, *The Administration of the Diocese of Worcester in the First Half of the Fourteenth Century* (Church Historical Society, 1965)

Hamilton Thompson, A, *The English Clergy and their Organization in the Later Middle Ages* (Oxford, 1947)

Offer, C J, *The Bishop's Register* (London, 1929) Includes extracts in translation.

Owen, D M, *The Records of the Established Church in England* (British Records Association, Archives and the User, no 1, 1970) A good brief summary, which describes the process by which the typical contents of the medieval register were later subdivided among a variety of files and other records.

Smith, D M, *Guide to Bishops' Registers of England and Wales* (Royal Historical Society, 1981). Lists all registers from the beginning to 1646, with a summary of their contents and valuable bibliography, including details of published registers.

Swanson, R N, *Catholic England* (Manchester, 1993) Includes extracts from registers in translation.

Swanson, R N, *Church and Society in Late Medieval England* (Blackwell, Oxford, 1989)

The 1669 Return of Nonconformist Conventicles

David L Wykes

ORIGIN

The survey or Return of Conventicles completed during the summer of 1669 on the instructions of Archbishop Sheldon is the most important source available for studying the earliest period of religious dissent after the Restoration, because, with the exception of the Quakers, only a handful of records belonging to dissenters survive from this period. Modern religious dissent dates from the Restoration religious settlement and the passing of the 1662 Act of Uniformity. Existing Elizabethan and early Stuart statutes were invoked to enforce attendance at the established church and further legislation was passed to suppress nonconformist meetings. The 1664 Conventicle Act made it unlawful for more than five people aged 16 and over, besides the household, to 'be present at any Assembly, Conventicle, or Meeting' for religious worship other than that of the Church of England. The statute remained in force until I March 1669, and it was in connection with the passing of a new act that Sheldon ordered his enquiry in June 1669. As the first comprehensive survey of nonconformist meetings the returns provide an invaluable account of the state of dissent during this crucial early period.

LOCATION AND FORMAT

An edition 'verbatim et literatum' of the majority of the surviving returns was published 80 years ago by Professor Lyon Turner from a manuscript volume in the Lambeth Palace Library. Although some of the returns from the volume have been published separately in local journals, this edition provides the most accessible source for the historian. The coverage of the Lambeth volume is not complete, but it contains evidence for nearly three-quarters of the dioceses in England and Wales, though unfortunately even for the dioceses that are included the evidence is often patchy and far from perfect, resulting in some cases in the omission of an entire archdeaconry. A copy of the returns for at least one of the missing archdeaconries, that of Northampton, has however survived and it is possible that others may be found locally. The Lambeth volume is a summary of the information collected at the parish level by the archdeacons, which was

Right, entry for part of the Nottingham Deanery, Archdeaconry of Nottingham (extract from *Original Records of Early Nonconformity Under Persecution and Indulgence*, ed. G.L. Turner (London, 1911) I, pp154-5).

Parishes & Conventicles in them	Sects	Numbers	Quality	Heads and Teachers
[279.] Eastwood i a monthly meeting of Greasley At the house of George Lane, a Tanner	Quakers	about 40		
Burton Jover i At the house of John Trewman every Sunday	nonco[n]formists & Presbyterians	about 100		Mr Robert Smalley
Mansfeild Woodhouse i At the house of Richard Bingham		about 8 families 10 or 12 psons more some of the best sort		The said John Trewman
Mansfield 3 first are 2nd	Quakers	about 13	meane	
3rd the papists meete at the houses of Samuel Clay & of Henry Dawes. the Quakers att the house of Timothy Garland. the Presbyterians meete att the houses of Mr John Whitlock, Mr Willm Reynolds, Mr Robert Porter, Mr John Billingsley & Mr Robert Smalley.	Papists Quakers Presbyterians	about 20 sometimes 60 not 20, on the weeke days but on Sundayes 40 or 50	meane persons better quali- tie than the rest.	Mr Turner & Mr Clay the Quakers are all Speakers The Presbyterian Speakers are the said Mr John Whitlock Mr William Reynolds Mr Robert Porter
[279b] Skigby 2 I. Att the house of Elizabeth Hutton widow Another att Mrs Lindley's 2 house.	Quakers Anabaptists & fifth monarchy men.			

then collated and forwarded by their bishops. Although the summary involves some loss of detail, a comparison with the original parish certificates which survive for the Archdeaconry of Leicester suggests that the losses are not significant.

CONTENT AND USES

The returns provide details on the number, size and distribution of the conventicles, and in most cases the preacher, denomination and host responsible for each meeting. Although historians have used the information on the numbers and size of conventicles the most widely, it is important to understand the underlying problems in using the evidence. Not only are the estimates of differing quality, but the wide variations in the type and even the dates when the conventicles were held makes any attempt to arrive at overall totals unrealistic. Besides the human problem of having to rely upon the clergy for estimates of numbers, and that some conventicles almost certainly remained undetected, it is clear that the returns are not a census, but a record of the incidence of conventicles, not all of which were active at the same time. Matthew Clark, for example, is reported as preaching in 14 Leicestershire parishes in 1669. Although he was undoubtedly one of the most active of the early nonconformist ministers, the number of places and the distances involved mean that it is impossible that he was preaching in all these parishes at the same time, rather that the returns record not only the places where he was still actively preaching, but also those where he had preached sometime in the past, perhaps only on a single occasion.

The returns provide invaluable evidence on the organisation of dissent in this period. A number of conventicles recorded in 1669 were already settled meetings from which it is possible to trace the history of the later congregations, but others were clearly less regular or organised and many parishes seem to have been unable to support constant preaching. Some conventicles reported were probably no more than a single improvised meeting occasioned by the appearance of a visiting preacher or the initial enthusiasm of a householder offering a place for worship. It is clear early religious dissent often consisted of little more than small, fluctuating pockets of nonconformity, which, depending upon the level of local support or the pressure of persecution, appeared or disappeared into the anonymity of the parish. In Northamptonshire there is evidence that conventicles were held by course on successive Sundays in neighbouring parishes, either as an attempt to avoid persecution or as part of the church's evangelical efforts to bring the gospel to a wider audience by taking the meeting to them. Many individuals also attended more than one meeting. The extract for Nottinghamshire illustrates the difficulties of using the figures for the number of attenders, because of the variety of descriptions used, and any attempt to provide overall figures of the number of conventicles and the numbers attending them is clearly impossible. Nonetheless, the returns are of value in determining the relative strength of the different denominations, particularly on a regional basis.

There are similar problems with the denominational descriptions used in the returns. Before the early eighteenth century, in many parts of the country

Presbyterians and Independents met together in one meeting, and conventicles described as either Presbyterian or Independent contained supporters of both groups. Denominational labels in this period tended to be very fluid, and when dissenters were few a meeting would include individuals of differing religious opinions who might not belong to the same denomination as the minister. Only where dissent was strong were Presbyterians and Independents able to support separate meetings. In contrast, a history of conflict between Baptists and Quakers, particularly over attempts to recruit each other's members, had led to a stricter division between the groups. The Anglican authorities were, however, less concerned with identifying the denomination responsible for the conventicle, though a record of hostility towards the sects makes it likely that in general Quakers and Baptists were correctly identified.

Sheldon also required information on the condition or status of the hosts and those who attended the meetings. This information does appear to have been open to a significant level of bias, with the authorities tending to stress the meanness and low condition of the individuals involved. The licences obtained under Charles II's Declaration of Indulgence in 1672 confirm that many of those who supported Presbyterian (and to a lesser extent Independent) meetings by licensing their own houses were of yeoman, tradesman and even gentry status. The evidence from the individuals presented at Quarter Sessions for attending conventicles suggests that those attending Quaker meetings were mainly craftsmen and husbandmen, but with a few yeomen and tradesmen. Baptist conventicles seemed to have lacked even the small number of more substantial figures generally found in Quaker meetings, but were by no means of the inferior status implied in the returns. Nonetheless it is difficult to be certain about the evidence from Quarter Sessions as those prosecuted for attending conventicles tended to be the wealthier supporters, who acted as hosts or teachers, who could pay the fines and were therefore worth prosecuting. In contrast, the women and labourers cited by the returns may frequently have been ignored by the parish constables and informers. The comments on social status are of most use when comparing denominations.

The value of the returns clearly depends upon their accuracy and reliability. Within the limitations inherent in any official survey of illegal activity, the results are in general satisfactory. The knowledge that the authorities had about many conventicles is impressive. They were invariably able to name the teachers and the host for each conventicle, even if the details concerning the size of the meeting or number of attenders were less accurately recorded or known. Although Quarter Sessions records provide references to conventicles not recorded in the returns, this does not necessarily invalidate the latter, since meetings which had been successfully prosecuted may well have disappeared by the time the survey was made or may never have been more than occasional meetings. The main value of the returns for the historian is at the county or national level because they allow comparisons between denominations and different parts of the country. Nonetheless, the evidence is descriptive rather than statistical. The returns are only a record of the conventicles known to the authorities and not a survey of the extent of the support for dissent. Some conventicles may have escaped the notice of the authorities, while in other cases the meeting recorded may already have been suppressed. In addition to the information about the conventicles themselves, the returns also help to identify the ministers and teachers who were active in promoting dissent, and in particular record the efforts of the ejected ministers. The returns can therefore be used to help detect the parishes where nonconformists were active. The value of the returns undoubtedly lies in the fact that they provide the first comprehensive survey of nonconformist meetings since the Restoration religious settlement: an account of the state of religious dissent after the first Conventicle Act and the attempts to suppress public meetings. They therefore provide the most important source for the study of the early history of dissent. But for the survey historians would have little idea of the size of individual conventicles or the relative strength of the different denominations. Indeed for some counties there is no alternative source as none of their Quarter Sessions records survive for this period.

BIBLIOGRAPHY

Archbishop Sheldon's manuscript volume which provides a summary of the Returns is in the Lambeth Palace Library, London: Lambeth MS639, fos 139-294, MS951/1, fos 111-113. The Returns are most readily available in the published edition edited by **Turner, G L**, *Original Records of Early Nonconformity Under Persecution and Indulgence* (London, 1911-14), 1, pp 3-176, 1, pp 823-28. In addition, the original certificates for the Archdeaconry of Leicester and a fair copy of the certificates for the Archdeaconry of Buckingham, which survive amongst the records of the Bishop of Lincoln and which include much valuable additional detail, have also been published by Evans and Broad (see below).

For examples of local editions, see **Evans, R H**, 'Nonconformists in Leicestershire in 1669', *Transactions of the Leicestershire Archaeological Society, XXV* (1949) pp 98-143; **Jewson, C B**, 'Return of Conventicles in Norwich Diocese, 1669 - Lambeth MS No.639', *Norfolk Archaeology*, XXXIII (1962), pp 6-34; *Bishop Fell and Nonconformity: Visitation Documents from the Oxfordshire Diocese, 1682-83*, ed. Clapinson,M,(Oxfordshire Record Society, LII, 1980); *Buckinghamshire Dissent and Parish Life, 1669-1712* (ed) **Broad, J**, Buckinghamshire Record Society, XXVIII (1993).

For studies of dissent that use the conventicle returns, see **Nuttall, G F**, 'Dissenting Churches in Kent before 1700', *Journal of Ecclesiastical History*, XIV (1963), pp 175-89; **Spufford, M** 'The Dissenting churches in Cambridgeshire from 1660 to 1700', *Proceedings of the Cambridgeshire Antiquarian Society*, LXI (1968), pp 67-95; **Wykes, D L**, 'The Church and Early Dissent: The 1669 Return of Nonconformist Conventicles for the Archdeaconry of Northampton', *Northamptonshire Past and Present*, VIII (1991-92), pp 197-209

34
Probate Accounts
Jacqueline Bower

The Accompte of John Spaine sonne and Administrator of all and singuler the goods Cattells Chattells and debts of Thomas Spaine late ... of the parish of Knowlton in the County of Kent Yeoman deceased By him made and personallie Declared the 24th day of December Anno Domini 1629 ...

First this Accomptant and Administrator Doth Charge himselfe with all and singuler such goods Cattells Chattells and debts as late were the said Deceaseds ... All which ... are contained and specified in an Inventory ... and doe in the whole extend and amount ... unto the summe of £982 5s

And this Accomptant sheweth and declareth that ... hee ... hath necessarilie paid and laid out ... in and about the Administring of the said deceased's goods ... the particuler summes of money hereunder mentioned ...

For 170 pound of beefe the second weeke of harvest £1 11s 10d

For mending the waggons and Courts and for other Carpenters worke done about the husbandry implements ... 6s

To Robert Spaine the said deceased's sonne for thrashing 72 seames of wheate... £3 12s

For carrying six quarters of wheate to Sandwich to bee sold ... 2s

To Mr Thomas Hales of the parish of Beaksborne the said Deceaseds landlord for rent of the house and land the said deceased dwelt and dyed in due and owing to him by the said deceased ... £720

(Centre for Kentish Studies, Kent Archives, PRC2/30/119)

ORIGIN

In the early modern period, after a person had died, it was the responsibility of the next of kin to compile a probate inventory, which supposedly listed all the deceased's moveable assets, such as clothing, household goods and furnishings, crops, livestock and leasehold property. The purpose of the inventory was to provide a record of the deceased's assets to prevent dishonesty by the executor or administrator and to assist him or her in discharging the deceased's outstanding financial obligations and distributing his estate to the next of kin. After the inventory had been made, it was submitted to the appropriate ecclesiastical court. The court then granted probate, if the deceased had left a will, or letters of administration if he or she had died intestate. The executor or administrator then gathered in any remaining assets of the deceased and paid all his outstanding debts. The administrator also settled any expenses which had been incurred since the deceased's death. During this period, the administrator kept a careful and detailed account of the money laid out from the estate. Accounts thus kept are known as probate accounts or administrators' accounts.

LOCATION AND FORMAT OF ACCOUNTS

The final stage in the process was for the completed account to be exhibited in the ecclesiastical court. It is not clear whether all ecclesiastical courts routinely kept copies of all accounts, or whether some courts only filed copies when there was some dispute over an estate, or not at all, but survival of accounts today is patchy, and they do not exist in such large numbers as probate inventories. In most dioceses, probate accounts survive from about 1570 to about 1720, although they were kept in the Diocese of York until 1858. The best collection is that for the Diocese of Canterbury, where about 13,500 probate accounts survive. As with most ecclesiastical court records, probate accounts, where they survive, are now generally held in county record offices. Those relating to estates dealt with by the Prerogative Court of Canterbury are held at the Public Record Office. Most county record offices now have indices to their own collections of probate accounts, and a complete index to surviving accounts in England and Wales is to be published by the British Record Society.

Probate accounts, being legal documents, follow a set format. The preamble names the administrator or executor, that is, the person responsible for compiling the account. The relationship of administrator to deceased is normally stated in the preamble or can be deduced from information in the body of the document. The name and parish of the deceased are given in the preamble, and sometimes his or her occupation or status. The date on which the account was presented to the court often follows.

The second paragraph of a probate account is a statement of the charge, or gross value of the estate. This is normally a common form statement of the inventory value. After the statement of the charge comes the body of the account in which the administrator details the various sums expended by him or her from the estate since the deceased's death. The first item entered in the account is normally the cost of the deceased's funeral, followed by costs incurred in the deceased's last sickness. Other expenses, such as settlement of wages, bills and debts not paid by the deceased in his lifetime, are listed in detail. Thus a probate account may contain information on the cost of such things as thatching a roof, shoeing a horse or ploughing a field, or, in more unusual accounts, the cost of attempting to salvage a boat, bringing to trial a murderer or feeding a household shut up during an outbreak of plague.

If the deceased left minor children, a major responsibility of the administrator was to see to their upbringing. The children's board and lodging, education, clothing and apprenticeship all had to be paid for from their deceased parent's estate, and all such expenditure was recorded in the account, down to the cost of mending shoes, knitting stockings and purchasing schoolbooks.

At the end of the account, the amount spent by the administrator was totalled and the result, the discharge, deducted from the charge to give the balance or net value of the estate. Quite frequently, the discharge exceeded the amount of the charge. The account would then end with a negative balance, or 'in surplussage'.

If the deceased had not left a will, it was the court's duty to distribute the balance among the next of kin. The manner of the distribution was detailed at the foot of the document. Everyone who received a share was named and his or her relationship to the deceased stated. Where married daughters were involved, the names of sons in law were often given, and the ages of all minor children stated.

USES OF PROBATE ACCOUNTS

Because they contain so much varied detail on all aspects of the lives of the middling and lower classes in town and country in the early modern period, there are many ways in which probate accounts can be used by economic, social and family historians. Family historians may find within individual accounts invaluable information both on their lineage and on the wealth, business affairs and standards of living of their forbears.

Probate accounts are important as a complementary source for probate inventories. While inventories give details of money owed to the deceased, they do not list debts owed by him. Assessments of average wealth of different social groups or within different regions based on information in probate inventories are thus almost certainly over-estimated. Because probate accounts list debts owed by the deceased, they give a more realistic impression of wealth in the early modern period than that derived from probate inventories. Used in conjunction with inventories, probate accounts can thus aid research into wealth and living standards in the early modern period. Information on rent can shed light on land values, and details of debts owed by the deceased can provide information on sources of credit in the early modern period.

To date, our knowledge of seventeenth century plague epidemics has chiefly been based on statistics derived from parish registers, material arising from official responses to epidemics, and diarists such as Evelyn and Pepys. Probate accounts, by listing the expenses of keeping households shut up for weeks or months at a time, plus payments for medical attention and nursing, give an insight into the experience of ordinary people during an epidemic.

Whereas values placed on goods in probate inventories represent what the appraisors thought the goods might fetch in a sale, prices for goods in probate accounts are a statement of what was actually paid, and therefore more likely to be accurate. Detailed study of wages and prices paid for goods in the late sixteenth and early seventeenth century may shed light on the local progress and effects of the Price Revolution of the period.

Probate accounts reveal details of housekeeping and family life in the early modern period which are available nowhere else. From the details of food purchased for the funeral feast and for consumption by the deceased's family and servants one can build up a picture of the diet enjoyed by different social classes — for example, whether beer or wine was drunk at a funeral — and the price and availability of various commodities at different dates and in different regions. Similarly, probate accounts contain detailed information of the clothing purchased for children of different social classes, and on the prevalence of the custom of 'placing out' children at very young ages.

As yet, probate accounts are a relatively little known and little used source. In counties where they survive, however, they should be as routinely consulted by historians as wills and probate inventories.

BIBLIOGRAPHY

Gittings, Clare, *Death, Burial and the Individual in Early Modern England* (1984)

Erickson, Amy Louise, 'An Introduction to Probate Accounts' in Spufford, Peter and Martin, G H (eds), *The Records of the Nation* (1990)

Spufford, Margaret, 'The Limitations of the Probate Inventory' in Chartres, John and Hey, David (eds), *English Rural Society 1500-1800* (1990)

Bower, Jacqueline, 'Probate Accounts as a Source for Kentish Early Modern Economic and Social History', *Archaeologia Cantiana CIX* (1991.)

Census Returns in England and Wales

Edward Higgs

THE ORIGINS AND NATURE OF CENSUS TAKING

A census has been taken in England and Wales every ten years since 1801, with the exception of 1941. The decennial enumerations from 1801 to 1831 were organised by John Rickman, a clerk of the House of Commons. Rickman was essentially concerned to discover the size of the population and whether it was expanding or contracting. To this end he asked the overseers of the poor to provide information on the numbers of men, women, families and houses in their parishes. Information on the number of individuals employed in agriculture, handicrafts, and all other employments was also sought. Later this information was collected for the number of families so engaged. More detailed questions relating to ages and occupations were posed in 1821 and 1831 respectively. At the same time Rickman asked the local clergy to provide him with information relating to baptisms, marriages and burials from the parish registers. In order to supply these head counts some overseers undertook far more detailed local investigations down to the level of named individuals.

On Rickman's death in 1840, the organisation of the decennial census was taken over by the General Register Office (GRO). The GRO had been set up in 1837 to undertake the civil registration of births, marriages and deaths. For this purpose the whole of the country had been divided into registration districts, each with a local registrar to handle the recording of such vital events and to send copies of the resulting certificates to the GRO in London. These were indexed to form a record of lines of descent as a means of establishing property rights, and analysed to generate medical data on causes of death and other statistics.

For the purposes of taking the census, each registration district was divided into enumeration districts of about 250 houses and a temporary enumerator appointed for each. It was the duty of the latter to hand each householder a household schedule on which they were to provide information on the members of their household on census night. This was usually a Sunday in March or April. There were also special census schedules for large institutions and, from 1851, forms for shipping. These were to be filled out by the heads of institutions and the captains of ships. The enumerators collected the household schedules for their district and copied them into books. These were then sent to a temporary Census Office in London run by the GRO, where the data was abstracted, tabled and published in Parliamentary Papers. From 1911 onwards the household schedules themselves formed the raw data from which abstraction was undertaken.

The Victorian GRO was predominantly interested in census data for medical and actuarial purposes. It believed that the incidence of disease was directly correlated with population densities and with the materials upon which people worked. The censuses, therefore, sought information on the numbers of people, families and houses (inhabited, uninhabited, or being built) in defined administrative areas; the determinants of family formation (age, sex, marital condition, relationship to head of family); birthplaces (both parish and country) as a proxy for migration; and occupations, especially modified by the materials being worked up. Householders were also asked to supply medical information on the incidence of blindness, deaf and dumbness, and, later, mental deficiencies. The census of 1841 was more limited in the scope and detail of the information it required, whilst new questions such as on employment status, rooms inhabited and home working were introduced from 1891 onwards. Information was also sought from employers on the number of hands employed, whilst farmers were asked to indicate the acreage farmed. Special welsh language household schedules were issued in Wales, and a question on language spoken by individuals was introduced into the principality in 1891.

LOCATION AND ACCESS

Since the returns of the censuses of 1801 to 1831 were published verbatim in Parliamentary Papers, the originals were destroyed at the beginning of this century. Some of the detailed parish enumerations have survived in local record offices.

The original householders' schedules of the censuses from 1841 to 1901 were destroyed in the Census Office after they had been used to check the entries in the enumerators' books. The enumerators' books for this period and the household schedules from 1911 onwards are held until they are 100 years old by the National Statistical Office, which incorporates the GRO. They are then transferred to the Public Record Office (PRO) and made available to the public on microfilm at the PRO's Family Records Centre, 1 Myddleton Street, London, EC1 1UW. Many local record offices and libraries have purchased microform copies of the returns for their area from the PRO. A guide to the distribution of such copies can be found in Gibson's *Census returns 1841-1881 on microfilm: a directory to local holdings.*

A computerised two percent sample of the 1851 census, and anonymised data from modern censuses, are held at the Data Archive at the University of Essex, Wivenhoe Park, Colchester, Essex, CO4 3SQ.

FORMAT

Each complete enumerator's book for households has pages at the beginning for a description of the enumeration district; summary tables of the numbers of houses, occupiers and persons on pages, and later in administrative divisions; summary tables for information on temporary changes in the size of the area's population; an example of how to fill in the book; and a declaration signed by those involved in collecting the data. In the case of the 1841 census, the summaries and declarations are at the back of the enumerator's book.

The pages for inserting nominal data then follow. At the top of each page is information on the administrative areas covered therein. Working from left to right across the page are columns for household schedule numbers, addresses, inhabited status of houses, and the information relating to individuals. Again, the 1841 census does not have schedule numbers. The census page is ruled into rows, one for each individual, and the information for each person, starting with their name, runs across the page. The individuals are grouped into households with a household head at the top, typically followed by spouse, offspring, other relations, servants, boarders, and so on. Households are then grouped in houses if they share such accommodation. Special marks, lines across the page in 1851 and oblique slashes at other dates, mark off the households and houses.

The schedules for large institutions are like those for households, although lacking the columns for schedule number, addresses, status of house, and the like. The shipping schedule is similar but gives details of the ship on the front cover. The schedule for institutions and ships are usually appended to the end of the household schedules for the enumeration district in which they lay on census night.

USES OF THE RECORDS

The census records are a unique source in terms of their comprehensiveness and the number of different dimensions within which people are placed. The census returns for each person and household are also in a highly standardised and structured form. They therefore lend themselves to statistical and computer analysis. The presence of names from 1841 onwards enables the census records to be linked to other nominal sources.

Since everybody was, at least in intent, included in the census, it is possible to reconstruct the aggregate characteristics of populations. With the identification of named individuals from 1841 onwards, it is also a prime source for family history, especially since the information on birthplaces can lead one back to parish registers.

The census places named individuals both socially, spatially and temporally. People are placed in households and, from 1851, are given a relationship to the head of the family. The source can thus be used to establish the structure of families and the forms of cohabitation. The influence of the family on matters such as occupational succession can also be studied. Occupational data and the presence of domestic servants in the household have also been used as proxies for social class.

Since individuals and families are placed in houses with addresses and in administrative areas, we can reconstruct the population geographically. It is thus possible to trace differences in family, age, occupational and social structures, and so on, between regions, parts of the same town, and even between adjacent streets. Since the census gives place of residence as well as of birth, it can be used to give some idea of the migration of individuals and families. The relationships between habitations, family structure and overcrowding can also be worked out for local housing markets.

As the census is taken every ten years, it is also possible to use the source to study individuals, families and areas across time. The life history of an individual or family can be reconstructed, as can the changing structure and nature of the population of parishes, towns, cities, regions and the country as a whole. Thus, shifts in national occupational structures over time, derived from the published *Census reports*, form one of the principle data series for reconstructing economic change.

The information in the enumerators' books must, however, be used with some caution. The strict reliability of certain elements of the data, especially ages, medical condition and the occupations of women and children, is in some doubt. Similarly, changes in the way in which certain entities were defined, households for example, makes comparison across time somewhat problematical. It should also be remembered that the census was only taken on one night, every ten years. The taking of the census in Spring almost certainly precluded the recording of much seasonal labour, especially that associated with the harvest. Data collected on census night might also reflect quite temporary local conditions. Thus, the low number of houses being built in 1891 probably reflected the severity of the previous Winter, which reduced the number of house starts, rather than long-term trends in the housing market.

BIBLIOGRAPHY

Glass, D V, *Numbering the People: the Eighteenth Century Population Controversy and the Development of Census and Vital Statistics in Britain* (1978)

Gibson, J S, *Census Returns 1841-1881 on Microfilm: a Directory to Local Holdings* (1990)

Higgs, Edward, *A Clearer Sense of the Census. The Victorian Censuses and Historical Research* (1996)

Lawton, R (ed) *The Census and Social Structure: an Interpretative Guide to Nineteenth Century Census for England and Wales* (1978)

Lumas, S, *Making Use of the Census* (1992)

Mills, D & Pearce, C, *People and Places in the Victorian Census* (1989)

Mills, D & Schürer, K, *Local Communities in the Victorian Census Enumerators' Books* (1996)

Nissel, M, *People Count: a History of the General Register Office* (1987)

Office of Population Censuses and Surveys & General Register Office, Edinburgh, *Guide to Census Reports, Great Britain 1801-1966* (1977)

Wrigley, E A (ed) *Nineteenth-century Society* (1972)

The Lloyd George Finance Act Material

Brian M Short

[Valuation Office surveyor's notes made in Field Book for Court Lodge Farm, Penhurst, East Sussex — from PRO IR 58/29199]

Farmhouse A very old fashioned house part built of stone & tile & part of brick, weather-tile & tile. Well blt.
Accom:— porch, *Grd floor*. Kitchen, small Sitting Room, large front Room (very bad Repr!) Pantry & Scullery & Cellar underground.
1st floor. Landing, 1 front bed all oak panelled, 4 bedrooms
Top. 2 attics (no use for bedrooms). Good Repair.
2 Cottages. A pair of semi-detached Cottages well built of Brick, Stucco & Tile.
Accom. of each Living Room & Washhouse & 3 bedrooms. Fair Repair

[We are also informed that Court Lodge Farm comprised agricultural land, house and buildings and cottages; it was 109 acres 2 roods 30 perches in extent; the occupier was C. White Senr; the owner the Earl of Ashburnham; agent A.P. Ashburnham-Clement; the farm was freehold on a yearly tenancy at £90 rent; that tithe of £17.5.4d was paid by the owner who also paid the insurance and was liable for repairs, the occupier paying other rates and taxes. An accompanying sketch map in the Field Book showed that the farm complex also included a brick, timber and tile cart lodge; a brick and tile 3-stall stable; a brick and tile store room and granary over loose box and lean-to meal room and brick and tile oast kiln; a timber and corrugated iron lean-to cow lodge and yard; a brick, timber and tile pig pound; a range of brick and tile open cow lodges and yards; a large brick, timber and tile barn and lean-to cow lodge; and a brick and tile lean-to cart lodge. All were referred to as in 'fair repair'.]

BACKGROUND

Under the provisions of Part I of the Finance (1909-10) Act 1910, a full survey of landownership in the United Kingdom as of April 1909 was mounted. This has become known as the Lloyd George 'Domesday', forming one element of his well-known attack on the landed interest, and helping to create the political storm surrounding the Liberal Chancellor's 'People's Budget'.

The resulting documentation was complex, and attention here will be devoted to that emanating from the proposed collection of Incremental Value Duty. This was to be a 20 per cent tax for central government levied on any increase in values

Extract from a 25-inch OS Map coloured as

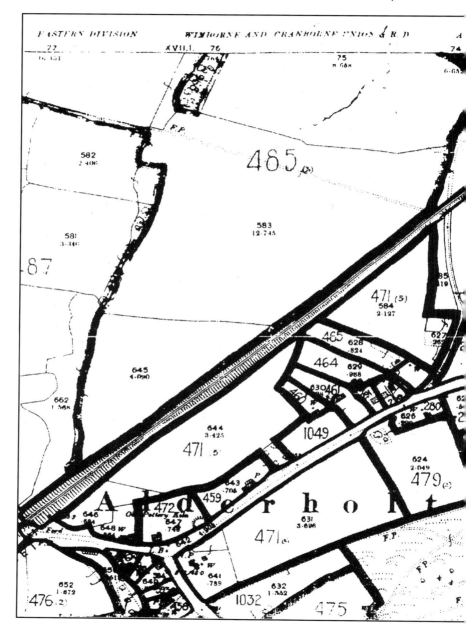

910: the Parish of Aldershot (Hants).

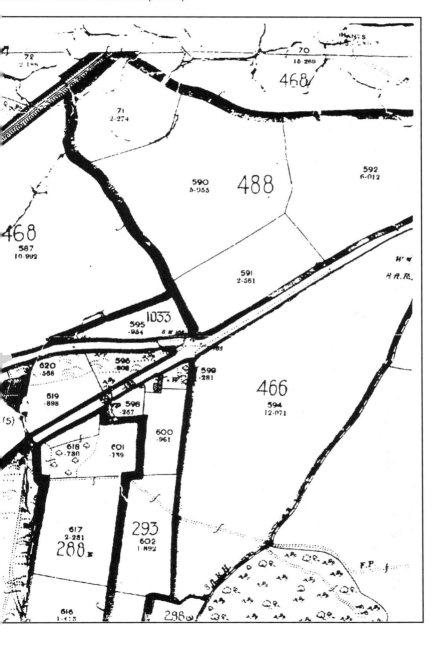

resulting from the sale or other transfer of property at any time subsequent to 1909. While many types of property were exempted from payment, nevertheless all property was to be made the subject of a survey, thereby fanning the flames of landed suspicion that this might be the basis for future more swingeing taxation, or even land nationalisation. Parts of the original Act were modified in subsequent years, and landowners combined in organisations such as the Land Union to combat the valuation and duties. After a number of humiliating reverses in the courts and following the hiatus of war, a Select Committee was appointed to investigate the 1910 duties, and although its report was itself inconclusive, the land clauses and most of the land duties of the Act were finally repealed in 1920.

THE FORMATION OF THE RECORDS AND THEIR LOCATION

The Inland Revenue quickly recruited staff to its District Valuation Offices (DVOs). The pre-existing 'Income Tax Parish' (ITP) was adopted as the basic unit for valuation purposes, with two or more civil parishes frequently uniting to form one ITP, and some 7,000 Land Valuation Officers (LVOs) appointed for each ITP across the country. Thus Leicestershire had 165 ITPs for about 328 Civil Parishes c 1910.

With the staff in post, the large-format Valuation Books (sometimes referred to as 'Domesday Books') were dispatched to the LVO in each ITP who arranged for the description of each property, together with names and addresses of owners and occupiers, and the figures for the extent of the property and its rateable value to be copied in from the Rate Book or 'Schedule A' registers. Any unrated properties were also added, and each hereditament within the ITP was given an identification number. Valuation Books survive for most areas, and are (with the exceptions of books for the City of London and Westminster (Paddington) which are in the Public Record Office (PRO)) to be found in county record offices or their equivalents.

Then, by August 1910, landowners across the country were sent the unpopular 'Form 4', on which they were to provide detailed information on every hereditament in their ownership. Subsequently deposited in the DVOs, most have now been destroyed. Form 4 contained owners' and occupiers' names and addresses, the address of the hereditament, the nature of the tenure and the name of the manor if copyhold, details of leases, and a description of the land and any buildings etc and the uses to which they were put, its area, rent obtained, outgoings such as taxes, tithes or any public rights to which it was subject, details of last sale (if any) within twenty years before 30 April 1909, and of subsequent expenditure, and questions about possible mineral rights.

Temporary Valuation Assistants were then posted to different parts of the Districts, armed with Field Books in which notes and calculations were made, and Ordnance Survey maps. The valuations were made following inspection of the property, and a set of values was then derived. No fewer than 95,000 volumes of the Field Books survive in the PRO. They are extant for most areas, although there are gaps, the extent of which is not yet known. They contain the fullest information of any of the 1910 documents. The entry for each hereditament comprised four pages in the book, with each book containing information on up to 100 hereditaments. All of the information from Form 4 was transcribed onto the first page of the Field Book entry for the hereditament, and the second page included a description of the property, which might include details of building materials, numbers and use of rooms, comments on repair and condition, as well as suitability for the purpose used, ancillary buildings and their condition, water supply and sanitary facilities etc. Comments on the state of cultivation, drainage, land use, etc, are common for farms. On the third page, sketch plans of farmsteads or industrial premises, traced from the Ordnance Survey sheets, gave details of buildings and their uses, although as work began to fall behind schedule in 1912 the sketches were dispensed with. The lower half of the second page and the final page include figures for the various values.

A statement of the provisional valuation results was next entered on Form 37, and a copy sent to the owner(s) of each hereditament and other interested parties. Forms 37 were retained in the DVOs and were made available to local repositories in 1979, but not all archivists took up the offer and they were only sporadically transferred. The Forms include the hereditament number, a description of the property, its situation, the name of the occupier and its extent. In addition they give the figures of each category of value and show how these were derived. On the reverse are the names and addresses of those persons to whom copies of the Provisional Valuation were issued.

To aid the valuation further, two sets of the largest scale Ordnance Survey sheets were made available (usually 1:2500, although 1:1250 or even 1:500 plans were used for built-up areas, and 1:10560 in many upland areas). One set was used as a working copy and the other as a permanent record. The boundaries of each hereditament were marked and its identification number entered onto the sheet. The Ordnance Survey agreed to make large-scale revisions for the valuation, especially where recent urban and industrial development had occurred. The permanent set of Record Plans, mounted on linen, has now been assembled in the PRO. The 'working copies', of uneven degrees of completeness and precision, generally contain less information than the Record Sheet Plans. They were offered to local repositories as long ago as 1968, where many still survive.

The Record Sheet Plans are crucially important. They should show the boundaries of the ITP in yellow, and the boundaries of each hereditament by a coloured edging or sometimes by an overall colour wash. The number of each hereditament was entered onto the plan in red. Detached portions should be braced together, and the various parts of the hereditament given a suffix to the main hereditament number e.g. Hereditament No. 263/1; 263/2 etc. This number corresponds to the hereditament number in the Valuation Book, and the key to finding the hereditament in the Field Books, through the PRO finding aids.

POTENTIAL USE OF THE RECORDS

The information to be found in the valuation documents presents numerous possibilities for the investigation of early twentieth century demography, society and economy.

The Lloyd George Finance Act Material

Firstly, the fact that the valuers were specifically concerned to identify owners of land for the purposes of taxation ensured the compilation of full data on owners' and occupiers' names and addresses and land and property ownership, at a time in the late Edwardian period of great significance for the landed estates. The identification of individuals and the study of landownership are among the most obvious uses of the data, and indeed the survey represents the most comprehensive set of property records ever compiled in the United Kingdom. With the addresses of owners given, it should be possible to make assessments as to the extent of owner-occupation of land and housing, absentee ownership, and possible family or kinship linkages. Since the Valuation Books were primarily copies of the Rate Book they will also compensate for the often considerable gaps in coverage of the latter in rural areas.

Secondly, each hereditament has its boundaries delineated and it follows that farm layout and fragmentation can be studied. Also of great importance is the study of tenure, the extent of freehold ownership, lease and copyhold details, rents and lengths of tenure.

Thirdly, there is much data on housing. The numbers and uses of rooms, house rents, sanitation and water supply, information on building materials, and details of stabling, pigsties and other buildings, repair and general condition etc should all be present, facilitating studies of living conditions in pre-World War I housing, illustrated graphically for all classes. Studies can also be made of land use in urban and rural areas. It is sometimes possible to examine rural land use on a field-by-field basis, though this cannot be predicted for any one area without consulting the relevant documents. It is also possible to study the industrial and commercial structure of towns and cities. The frequently detailed information regarding buildings and equipment enhances our knowledge of industrial, domestic and other buildings which have since been demolished or heavily altered.

Most of these topics can also be studied over time, and there are many possibilities for comparative work with other documents. Comparisons with the Tithe Surveys allows assessments to be made of changes in ownership and occupation structures, land-use patterns and farm fragmentation or consolidation from the beginning of Victoria's reign to the first World War.

Comparison with the 1891 census enumerators' schedules and relevant *Kelly's Directories* allows some limited house repopulation. Linkage with the 4 June agricultural returns is also an exciting prospect. Future comparisons might also use material derived from the local rate revaluation of the 1930s, and perhaps more importantly, with the National Farm Survey (1941-43) data. Researchers' ingenuity will uncover many more possibilities, and the development of computerised data bases and analyses will prove indispensable.

However, research on the valuation material can be frustrating, and there can be many unanticipated difficulties. Some of these problems originate in the way the valuation was originally conceived and framed, or in the instructions issued to valuation staff, or their sometimes idiosyncratic contemporary interpretation of instructions. Unfortunately, archival policies since the first documents reached the public domain in 1968 have created a third category of problem, relating to a lack of awareness of their true worth and their splitting up amongst several different repositories. Hopefully research will find a way around the first set of problems, and greater knowledge will help ameliorate the second.

BIBLIOGRAPHY

Foot, William, 'Maps for Family History', *Public Record Office Readers' Guide No.9* (1994)

Murray, B K, *The People's Budget 1909-10: Lloyd George and Liberal Politics* (Oxford, 1980)

PRO, Valuation Office: Records created under the Finance (1909-10) Act 1910, *Information Bulletin* 68 (1988)

Short, Brian, Reed, Mick and Caudwell, William, 'The County of Sussex in 1910: Sources for a New Analysis', *Sussex Archaeological Collections*, Vol 125, pp.199-224 (1987)

Short, Brian, *Land and Society in Edwardian Britain* (Cambridge, 1997)

Assistant Poor Law Commissioners' Correspondence

Simon Fowler

I called at the Workhouse this Morning and though a perfect stranger, I was shown over the House by the Matron. I find it in good order, the Inmates appear to be healthy and exceedingly comfortable but I was grieved to find several Lunatics, Epileptics, and Idiots in the House these ought all to be removed to an Asylum their detention is highly disgraceful to all parties concerned most chiefly so to the Assistant Poor Law Commissioner.
MH 12/6470, no. 13390B, 22 September 1843
(Dr Begley [of Middlesex County Lunatic Asylum]: entry in Leicester Union Workhouse visitors' book)

Such has been the violence of some of the able-bodied men that they have disturbed the whole house; the aged and well conducted paupers have complained of the annoyance they have been subject to and it certainly was necessary to make a division of the able-bodied class and entirely to separate a portion of them from the other inmates of the House. One of this class was convicted at the last Spring Assizes of assaulting the master with intent to do him bodily harm and sentenced to fifteen years transportation.
MH 12/6471, no. 11848B, 22 August 1846
(Assistant Poor Law Commissioner Robert Weale to the Poor Law Commission)

BACKGROUND

Before 1834 there was no central direction or co-ordination of the relief of poverty. Each parish cared for the poor in its own way. Under Gilbert's Act of 1782 a few parishes, or groups of parishes, had set up workhouses, but most parishes depended on overseers elected annually to administer the poor law as they saw fit and with due regard to the interests of the Poor Rate payer. In the early years of the nineteenth century this system was beginning to break down under the weight of the tremendous changes caused by the industrial revolution and the resultant explosion in population which led to increasing financial pressures on parishes and rate-payers alike. A Royal Commission on the workings of the poor law was established in 1832. Its findings were very heavily influenced by Utilitarian thinkers, such as Edwin Chadwick and Nassau Senior, who argued that the system of allowances (out-relief) paid to paupers was both wasteful and an inducement to idleness, and that the solution was to put the poor in workhouses whose severity would induce all but the most incapacitated pauper to leave voluntarily and seek work.

The work of the Commission led to the Poor Law Amendment Act of 1834. With the exception of the existing Gilbert Unions, and a few other areas which already had local acts, poor law unions, comprising a number of neighbouring parishes, were established to administer the poor law locally, under the direction of elected boards of guardians. The intention was to introduce uniformity of treatment of paupers throughout England and Wales: unions were required to set up workhouses and appoint officials to administer the new Act. In practice it proved impossible to impose uniformity, although rigorous attempts were made to enforce it after 1871; under the New Poor Law as under the Old, policies adopted by guardians were based on local needs.

The New Poor Law was finally abolished in 1929, with effect from 1930, although some elements lingered on to 1948. The work of the poor law union and boards of guardians changed dramatically over this period. The union was at its most influential in the twenty years or so after 1871 when guardians had many powers, over sanitation and slum clearance for example, later transferred to boroughs and rural districts. The need for relief of the poor was at its most acute during the great depression of the 1840s; thereafter the number of paupers gradually declined relative to the population as a whole.

From 1834 until the abolition of the poor law in 1929 three government departments were responsible for its administration: the Poor Law Commission (1834-1847), the Poor Law Board (1847-1871) and the Local Government Board (1871-1919). The Local Government Board was renamed the Ministry of Health in 1919.

Three Poor Law Commissioners were appointed in 1834 to co-ordinate the work of the formation of poor law unions and to maintain direct contact with the new boards of guardians. By 1847 it was felt that the Commission was not suitable for the tasks before it; it was seen as insufficiently accountable to Parliament and there was general concern, after several well publicised scandals, that the Commission was not adequately supervising the work of poor law unions.

The Poor Law Board consisted of a President, holding ministerial rank, and other ministers; its work was carried out by the President with the assistance of a parliamentary secretary and a secretariat of civil servants, and its role become the supervision of boards of guardians and the inspection of workhouses rather than the formulation of an integrated system of poor relief.

The Local Government Board was the result of a merger in 1871 of the Poor Law Board, the Local Government Act Office of the Home Office (which had inherited the powers of the General Board of Health in 1858), and the Medical Department of the Privy Council Office, to form a single board with primary responsibility for the supervision of local government services. It comprised a President and a number of ex officio members, and poor law responsibilities were looked after by the Poor Law Department. The main duties of the Department were the supervision of poor law unions outside London and, from 1873, related medical services for the poor. In 1884 it took over responsibilities for the poor law in London from the Metropolitan Department.

LOCATION AND CONTENTS

Surviving records of the government departments responsible for the poor law are held by the Public Record Office at Kew. Many records, especially those for the period after 1900, were destroyed by enemy action in 1941 or by fire in 1944.

The most important class of records is the correspondence with poor law unions and local authorities; it is especially valuable because it contains much about the poor law locally which no longer survives elsewhere, and is particularly important for the period between 1834 and 1871. This correspondence is to be found in class MH 12. It is arranged by county and then by poor law union; the metropolitan unions are to be found together. The papers for each union are bound together in a series of 16,741 volumes, many of which are now in poor condition.

The quality of correspondence for each union varies. Files for some unions, such as Richmond (Surrey), contain much of value. Other volumes, Arundel for example, are disappointing. In general, as might be expected, the later the period the more detailed are the records. It is difficult to describe succinctly what the historian is likely to find in these papers. The supervising departments were interested in all aspects of the work of unions, although before the 1870s little attempt was made to influence directly what guardians did. In turn boards of guardians consulted Whitehall on matters on which they were not sure. There is also a little correspondence with individuals, including a few paupers, usually complaints about how guardians were functioning locally.

The Poor Law Commissioners and their successors sent out a stream of circulars to unions on a variety of subjects, copies of which are in MH 10. Replies are in MH 12, although many unions did not bother to respond to requests for information. At various times during the 1840s and 1850s, for example, unions were asked to send in dietaries for the various classes of paupers in their workhouses.

Assistant Poor Law Commissioners were appointed in 1834 to supervise the establishment of unions throughout England and Wales. After this task had been completed they continued regularly to inspect workhouses and act as a conduit of advice to and from the centre. They were renamed Poor Law Inspectors in 1847. They were often seriously over-worked with large areas to cover, but the Inspectorate increased in size after 1871 and became more specialist with separate inspectors for, amongst other subjects, engineering, medical and schools. A few women were appointed to the Inspectorate in the 1890s.

MH 12 may include reports from Assistant Poor Law Commissioners about the establishment of individual unions and their attempts to introduce the New Poor Law locally. Thereafter there is a lull, but many reports submitted by Poor Law Inspectors survive for the period after the mid-1840s. Inspectors normally submitted reports about the conditions of individual workhouses on pre-printed forms. Comments are usually brief but can be revealing especially if overcrowding or other faults are being discussed. Some correspondence with inspectors can be found in MH 32; this class is arranged under the name of individual inspectors rather than by poor law union. Reports prepared by inspectors are occasionally printed in the annual reports of the central authority.

Unions had the right to appoint officials, although this had to be approved centrally. MH 12 includes many forms completed by applicants for jobs and related paperwork about salaries and the creation of new posts. In addition Whitehall kept registers of paid officers in which were noted appointments by boards of guardians and other local authorities of administrative, professional and institutional staff. (These registers are in PRO class MH 9.)

During the early 1870s unions increasingly took on responsibilities for sanitation and slum clearance. The papers in MH 12 show this concern: they may include for example plans for slum clearance or for building a municipal bath house or other projects for municipal improvement. Although many of these powers were transferred to local authorities in 1894 papers on these subjects continue to be included.

If the union ran a workhouse school there will often be reports in MH 12 from Poor Law Inspectors about the quality of tuition and the abilities of the schoolmaster or mistress. A number of neighbouring unions sometimes combined to set up a joint school district, especially in the metropolitan area. As well as papers of individual unions in MH 12, records of some school districts are in class MH 17. They relate to the administration and control of district schools, including appointment of managers and teaching and nursing staff, inspection of schools, construction and finance of buildings, and medical services.

Unions occasionally combined to form asylum districts which were organised in a similar manner to school districts. Again correspondence relating to the control of the mentally ill is in MH 12, together with papers about the establishment of asylum districts. Papers of the Sick Asylum Districts, the Metropolitan Asylum Board, and other authorities in London only are in MH 17.

USE

MH 12 and its associated classes provide an unparalleled source for the administration of the New Poor Law in a particular union. They complement material held in local record offices and sometimes form the only source; usually minutes of boards of guardians are available, even if the multiplicity of other records is not, but in some cases, such as the Nottingham Union, not even the minutes survive.

BIBLIOGRAPHY

Crowther, M A, *The Workhouse System 1834-1929* *(1981)*

Digby, A, *The Poor Law in Nineteenth-century England and Wales* (1982, 2nd ed., 1989)

Fraser, D (ed) *The New Poor Law in the Nineteenth Century* *(1976)*

Rose, M E, *The English Poor Law 1780-1930* (Newton Abbot, 1971)

Rose, M E, *The Relief of Poverty 1834-1914* (1972, reprinted 1974)

Webb, S & B, *English Poor Law History, Part II: The last hundred years* (1929, reprinted 1963)

Wood, P, *Poverty and the Workhouse in Victorian Britain* (1991)

Public Record Office records relating to the New Poor Law are briefly described in the *Current Guide* (1992), which is available on microfilm in large libraries and at the PRO itself. MH 12 references for individual unions are included in **Jeremy Gibson** *et al*, *Poor Law Union Records* *(4* parts, 1993). This book also lists all known records of the boards of guardians held locally.

38
Pipe Rolls
David Crook

[From the pipe roll for the tenth year of King Richard I, Michaelmas 1198.]

NOTINGEHAM ET DEREBISCIR'

Willelmus Briewerre reddit compotum de CC et lxxix libris et v solidis et xj denariis blanc' et xl libris et x solidis numero de firma de Notingeham et Derebiscir'. In thesauro C et lxvij libras et v solidos et ix denarios blanc' et xl libras et x solidos numero.

Et in elemosinis constitutis mililtibus de Templo ij marcas. Et canonicis de Derebi x solidos. Et canonicis de Schirwud' v solidos in Papewich...

Et in operatione castelli de Notingeham l solidos per breve regis...Et in emendatione domorum in castello de Bulesoures viij solidos per idem breve. Et in emendatione gaiole de Notingeham x solidos per idem breve. Et pro ferramentis prisonum vj solidos per idem breve...

NOVA OBLATA

Willelmus de Lond' [*blank*] l marcas pro xij libratis terre unde dissaisitus fuit quia fuit in castello de Notingeham cum comite J....

Ivetta que fuit uxor Simonis filii Ricardi reddit compotum de xx solidis pro habendo recto de dote sua versus Radulfum filium suum in curia regis apud Westmonasterium. In thesauro dimidiam marcam. Et debet j marcam.

NOTTINGHAMSHIRE AND DERBYSHIRE

William Briewerre renders account of £279 5s 11d blanched [tested by assay] and £40 10s by tale [not tested] of the farm of Nottinghamshire and Derbyshire. In the treasury £167 5s 9d blanched and £40 10s by tale.

And in fixed alms granted to the Knights Templar 2 marks. And to the canons of Derby 10s. And to the canons of Sherwood [Newstead] 5s in Papplewick....

And in works on Nottingham castle 50s by the king's writ....And in repairs of the houses at Bolsover castle 8s by the same writ. And in repairs of Nottingham gaol 10s by the same writ. And for the fetters of the prisoners 6s by the same writ...

NEW OFFERINGS

William of London [*no response*] 50 marks for 12 librates of land [land worth £12 a year] of which he was disseised because he was in Nottingham castle with Count John.

Yvette widow of Simon son of Richard renders account of 20s for having right of her dower against her son Ralph in the king's court at Westminster. In the treasury half a mark. And she owes one mark.

ORIGIN, DURATION AND NAME

Pipe rolls are the earliest series of records of the English state. They contain the annual accounts made by the sheriffs of the counties before the barons of the Exchequer, the monarch's auditors, around the audit table of the Exchequer, the financial department of government, at Westminster. The process is described in the earliest treatise on English government, the *Dialogue concerning the Exchequer*, written by Richard Fitzneil, the treasurer, about 1177. The Exchequer, which derived its name from the chequered cloth which lay on the table and was used to make calculations through the use of counters, had certainly come into existence by the year 1110. A single early roll survives giving the accounts for the financial year running from Michaelmas (29 September) 1129 to Michaelmas 1130; then there is an almost unbroken series from the roll for 1155/56 to that for 1831/32, when the Exchequer ceased to be responsible for auditing the sheriffs' accounts. In all, the surviving pipe rolls cover a period of 703 years.

Officially known as the 'great roll' or the 'roll of the year', the annual roll had also become known as the 'pipe roll' by the middle of the fourteenth century. Each individual rotulus, comprising two large membranes of parchment sewn together head to tail to form a single sheet about 16 inches wide and roughly 5 feet long, had by about 1300 become known as the 'pipe' of a particular county, almost certainly because when rolled up it resembled a pipe. When sewn together at the head at the end of the year the pipes of several counties comprised the 'roll of pipes' or pipe roll. From the later twelfth century to 1368 they included, besides the sheriffs' accounts, the accounts of a variety of other officials administering other sources of royal income or items of expenditure, such as vacant bishoprics and abbeys, escheated lands, mints, castles and palaces, or even the expense accounts of royal messengers. Here we will consider only the county accounts, which provided the basic content of the rolls for the entire period of their existence.

LOCATION OF RECORDS

The records are held and are available for research at the Public Record Office in Ruskin Avenue, Kew, Richmond, Surrey, TW9 4DU. Their class reference is E 372, and the appropriate series number assigned to the roll for a particular year can be ascertained from the class list. The rolls for the period down to 1221, and for the Exchequer years 1229/30 and 1241/42, have been printed in full transcript, mostly by the Pipe Roll Society. For most of the period covered by the published editions, the rolls are the only series of government records, so virtually all the information they give is unobtainable from other sources; after about 1200 a great deal of information is available from other series of records which began at around that date. They are in Latin, apart from a brief period in the 1650s, until 1733.

THE COUNTY FARM

The basis of the sheriff's account was the farm, a fixed sum he paid to the king for the income from the king's lands and some judicial rights in the county. The amount was fixed by the reign of Henry II, and is given in the rolls from 1198 onwards, but its principal interest for most historians is rather in the information given in the allowances that the sheriff claimed against it for lands granted to subjects, which therefore yielded no income, or for expenditure he was authorised to make on the king's behalf, whether with or without the king's writ. (Expenditure on castles and prison allowed in the extract was authorised by writ.)

Because they rarely altered, the county farms were removed from the pipe roll in 1284 and placed in a separate 'roll of the bodies of the counties' (E 372/129). What remained were other, smaller, farms of cities and towns, manors, forests, fisheries and a variety of other smaller units which produced income for the king but which were not or were no longer part of the farm, and income of a non-recurring nature, such as the financial penalties imposed by the king's courts. These farms came to be the first main element in the county accounts from the point at which the county farms were removed right through to the end of the series in 1832. They are of interest in giving details of the crown lands and other sources of income granted at fee farm or leased to individuals.

In the early rolls the farms were followed by a middle section of the account containing old debts still owing, including old farms pushed further down the account by newer material being inserted above them. For the first few years they continued under the headings, if any, given to them when they first appeared, which became shortened and then disappeared, leaving an undifferentiated mass of old debts. Various means were used to prune the account of uncollectable debts during the thirteenth century, until in 1323 a new series of exannual rolls (E 363) was established to hold such debts, now regularly removed from the pipe rolls. If payment was ever made, a debt was reinstated in the pipe roll for formal clearance. The surviving exannual rolls run as far as 1764.

The later parts of the account consisted in the earlier rolls of entries of income of an irregular nature, especially the profits of justice, offerings for the king's favour (like Yvette's above), and the proceeds of taxation. The first were records of the amercements (penalties) imposed by the king's justices, in eyre, of assize or of the forest, who visited the shires periodically, listed under headings containing the name of the leading justice or justices. Until the very end of the twelfth century none of the justices' own records of their proceedings have survived, and in the earlier part of the thirteenth century they are relatively rare, so the information in the pipe rolls is the only evidence available for many judicial visitations. The rolls are therefore of vital importance in the study of the legal history of that period. They later continued to carry the accounts for the penalties imposed in the itinerant courts, although in less detail, and the overall figures for penalties imposed in the central courts, the King's Bench and the Common Bench (later Common Pleas), which had come to dominate the legal system by 1300.

Offerings for the king's favour were at first listed under various headings, but by 1196 the heading 'Nova Oblata' (New Offerings) had become established. The earlier rolls included many colourful offerings, called fines, which illustrate in great detail the personal nature of government and the political relationship between the king and his major subjects. William of London lost his land because he supported Count John, soon to become king, in his rebellion against King Richard in 1194, and offered 50 marks to get it back. Later the heading 'Nova Oblata' was used to signal the beginning of all new material of a casual nature on the current roll, and, in its revised form 'New Matters' after the pipe rolls began to be written in English, remained a regular feature, following the small farms, until the series came to an end in 1832. The overall sums imposed as penalties by the central courts were among the debts which were included under it.

The earlier rolls contain the main surviving records of the older taxes, such as scutage (a tax on knights' fees) and tallage (a tax on boroughs and the king's own estate, the royal demesne). By the late thirteenth century they had been replaced by regular lay and clerical subsidies, general taxes whose accounts came to be recorded in a separate series of rolls physically similar to the pipe rolls (E 359), which began in 1275, while the accounts for the other main source of royal income, the customs, were from their beginning in 1275 recorded in another series of similar rolls (E 356). All the other foreign accounts not already recorded in separate rolls were removed in 1368 into a series of foreign accounts rolls (E 364). After that date new types of material were sometimes added to the county accounts, such as payments by the sheriff to justices of the peace for attending sessions, authorised by an act of 1388, and sums exacted from Catholic recusants for non-attendance at Anglican services under an act of 1581 (removed to two separate series of recusant rolls in 1592), but the main structure and form of the accounts remained basically unaltered for the remainder of their existence.

BIBLIOGRAPHY

Bowler, Dom H, introduction to 'Recusant Roll No. 2 (1593-1594)', *Catholic Record Society Record Series*, volume 57 (1965)

Johnson, C, (ed) *Dialogus de Scaccario* (Edinburgh, 1950)

Meekings, C A F, 'The Pipe Roll Order of 12 February 1270', in *Studies Presented to Sir Hilary Jenkinson*, ed Conway Davies, J (Oxford, 1957, pp222-53) reprinted in *Studies in Thirteenth Century Justice and Administration*, edited by Hunnisett, R F and Crook, D (London, 1981)

Mills, M H (ed) *The Pipe Roll for 1295, Surrey Membrane*, Surrey Record Society, volume 21, London, 1924, reprinted, 1968

Building Plans

Gillian Cookson

BACKGROUND AND ORIGIN

The power of local authorities to intervene in various aspects of local life was well established as early as the eighteenth century. These rights came from private Acts of Parliament and were especially used in the rapidly growing industrial towns, and with increasing frequency after 1800. The range of activities which could be regulated or controlled included making and repairing

Plan of proposed building of the Prince of Wales music hall, Leicester, 1889 (sheet 1) *Leicestershire Record Office*

highways; laying sewers and drains; installing street lights; setting up a police force; and also the control of buildings, especially to prevent obstructions or danger to the public. The privately sponsored Acts, though often of great local significance, were not without their problems; these included confusion over varying provisions in different areas, and poor drafting which meant that some of the regulations were unenforceable.

An awareness grew in the 1830s and 1840s of the link between public health and the condition of buildings. The cholera epidemics of those decades concentrated minds on the problem and a number of damning reports on the state of towns were produced. One of the results was the Public Health Act of 1848. This Act was hailed as a landmark, though councils were allowed, rather than compelled, to take action on building control. A number of local authorities took advantage of this opportunity, but the vast majority still did not. The Local Government Act of 1858 extended councils' powers, without a private Act being necessary. Bye-laws could be used to specify such details as type of building materials, thickness of walls, spaces between buildings, method of construction of drains, and so on. These specifications were not determined by Parliament, but were decided locally to conform, up to a point, with local customs and methods.

Some towns did not join in the new system until later. Into this category fall some of the old established corporations where private Acts were already in operation to control development; for example, Leeds did not start to operate a modern system of building controls until 1867.

FORMAT

Once the new scheme had been adopted, developers were required to submit plans for approval to a committee of the local authority. A copy of the plan was retained by the council for future reference. In towns of any size, the number of deposited plans quickly grew into thousands, and methods of storage and retrieval had to be devised.

The organisation of these deposited plans varies slightly from place to place. Usually a register was drawn up which listed the plans in the order of submission and numbered them in sequence. The register generally gives the following information: the name of the applicant, who could have been the owner, developer, architect or other agent; the street or streets in which the site was situated; a brief description of the proposal, which should indicate whether the scheme was to alter or extend an existing building; a plan number; the date of submission; a note of whether the plan was approved, and the date of the committee meeting at which it was considered. These registers can themselves be very informative even when the plans they list are lost or inaccessible.

Occasionally there is supplementary information available. For example, the records for Halifax contain a companion volume, 'Borough Surveyor's Reports to Improvement Committees', for the years 1872-99. These provide extra details of interest to a local historian, such as 'commenced building before depositing plans' or 'building on the site of old cottages'.

Many of the registers are also indexed, often by street, or by the name of the property owner. There are variations in the way the records have been kept; for example sometimes the plans themselves were filed alphabetically under the street or applicant's name, or arranged in chronological order, or even listed under a plot or map reference number. In most cases, though, plans were kept simply in numerical order.

The original plans vary widely in quality and condition. Some are on a durable linen-backed paper, and these tend to have weathered better than those drawn on tracing paper. The best sets of building plans are those for large and important new constructions, such as factories or public buildings; these would probably have been drawn by leading local architects, and include sections through the site, precise measurements and levels, details of the building's construction and materials, as well as plans and elevations.

LOCATION

Considering their bulk and the problems involved in storage, it is surprising that so many nineteenth century building plans have survived. Many are now deposited in local record offices, and any search should begin there. If the plans are not at the record office, it is likely that archivists there will know where they are.

In many cases the plans have been microfilmed for ease of access, and also in order to protect the originals, some of which are too fragile to use. The very act of opening a plan to photograph it may destroy it; other originals, considered to be of little interest or value in relation to the space they occupy, have been discarded after being copied. It should also be noted that some original plans have been lost, as these have been working documents in council departments for many years; it is often drawings which are potentially the most interesting which have disappeared. For example, plans by well known architects, or of notable buildings, tend to stray. One suspects that this loss may not always have been accidental, but the best and biggest sets of plans, those for large new buildings of the Victorian period, were often pulled out of sequence for perfectly legitimate reasons when alterations were made to the building, and can sometimes be found re-filed with the later application.

Where building plans survive and have not been lodged with record offices, they may be found with the successor of the local authority concerned, often in planning or building control department stores (they are occasionally still used as reference documents for modern building control applications), but sometimes in locations as inconvenient as cellars and attics of town and city halls. Some persistence may be necessary in order to obtain access; the furtherance of historical research is not necessarily a top priority for a busy planning officer.

USES OF THE RECORDS

It is not an exaggeration to say that building plans rank among the finest evidence for any study of the physical appearance of Victorian towns. Because they are so detailed, containing plans and sections along with elevations, these records make possible a minute reconstruction of urban scenes which may long since have disappeared.

Besides being an obvious source for any topographical or architectural study, the plans have applications for many other aspects of urban and industrial history. They can contribute to knowledge of the work of local builders, or standards of working class housing, the growth of public building, or the pace of commercial and industrial development.

One of their major virtues is that they contain very precise information about the date, location and construction of the building concerned. So for a particular site, say an industrial building subjected to many alterations as businesses expanded or technology changed, it is possible to be extremely accurate about when rebuilding or extension occurred and in what form. A precision is possible which even the most accomplished architectural historian could not achieve by looking at physical remains on the site. Information as specific as the internal arrangements of buildings and the exact use of rooms can be found on building plans; this kind of detail is rarely found elsewhere, for example on town plans or even Ordnance Survey maps.

Building control records contain more than just plans; often architects' drawings survive which illustrate the elevations of buildings which may have been long demolished. These can be as useful as, or better than, contemporary photographs for showing details of the facade of a building.

As with all historical records a note of caution should be sounded about the use of building plans. In view of the difficulties in finding where the plans are housed, it might be assumed that once the collection has been located, all problems are over. This is not the case.

The lists kept in record offices are usually over-optimistic about the numbers of the plans held. In many cases this seems to be because the archives are so vast that staff have not been able to do a full 'stock check'. So, often, odd plans are found to be missing: sometimes whole sequences, even years of plans have gone adrift, perhaps thrown away before they had become old enough to be interesting, or victim of a flood or other natural disaster in the planning department. This is obviously a matter of chance, though it does seem that survival rates for complete series are higher in the larger towns than in smaller rural and urban districts.

If the plan is where it should be, it may not be useable; those drawn on thin paper may have disintegrated into confetti. Others are durable but disappointing; they turn out to be amateurish drawings of minor alterations to buildings. If a plan has weathered well and looks promising, it can be awkward to work from; for any serious topographical history it is usual to obtain copies of visual material, but many of these plans are too big to trace and will not fit on a photocopier (though planning departments may have suitable specialised equipment). If the plan is in a record office, expensive arrangements may be necessary to have the plan photographed or photocopied. Copying problems also apply to plans on microfiche; 'hard' copies come off the machine on A4 sheets and have to be laboriously reassembled. In any case, a microfiche reader is hardly the ideal way to look at building plans as the whole plan rarely fits on a screen.

A final point to check is whether the development conformed to the drawing; in some cases, the plan was not proceeded with in full or at all. Building plans should therefore be compared as far as possible with surviving buildings or with other maps or photographic records.

BIBLIOGRAPHY

Cookson, Gillian, 'Large Scale Problems: The Neglect of Building Plans', *The Local Historian*, vol 19, no 1, February 1989, pp3-7

Gaskell, S Martin, *Building Control: National Legislation and the Introduction of Local Bye-Laws in Victorian England* (1983)

James, David, 'Building Plans', in Reeder, David (ed) *Archives and the Historian* (Leicester, 1989) pp51-79.

40

Ordnance Survey Maps

Richard Oliver

The maps of the Ordnance Survey have the reputation of being 'the best in the world'; be that as it may, the availability of OS mapping of a specified date and scale varies widely across Britain, and only a general summary can be given here. For further information this writer's *Ordnance Survey Maps: a concise guide for historians* should be consulted. Ordnance Survey Maps continue to be produced, and here only those produced for Great Britain before 1939 are considered.

There are four main groups of OS maps with which the historian needs to be concerned. In order of appearance they are:

1. The one-inch (1:63,360), (now replaced by the 1:50,000), introduced 1805.
2. The six-inch (1:10, 560), introduced 1840.
3. The 'town scales': five feet to one mile (1:1056), ten feet to one mile (1:528) and 1:500 (10.56 feet to one mile), introduced 1842, for urban areas only.
4. The 1:2500 (25.344 inches to one mile), introduced 1853.

Groups 1, 2 and 4 were progressively introduced as the largest scale of publication as the survey moved northwards, so that after 1840 the one-inch and after 1853 the six-inch were derived from larger-scale mapping.

As a rule of thumb, the larger the scale the more detailed the map, but also the less the number of editions. The four families will be discussed here therefore in diminishing order of scale.

1. The 'town scales'. Between 1842 and 1855 the standard scale of mapping for urban areas of 4000 population at the time of survey was the five feet. The distribution of towns mapped at this scale is similar to that of counties mapped at the six-inch scale at this time. A few of these five feet surveys were revised later in the century; most were replaced between 1887 and 1895 by 1:500 mapping. In 1848-50 a 'skeleton' survey, amounting to little more than a street plan, of London was made at this scale. Between 1862 and 1872 it was replaced by a conventional survey, which was revised in 1893-5. These maps were all published.

Between 1850 and 1856 about 30 towns were mapped by the OS at the true ten feet scale for public health purposes. Most of these plans include details of sanitary hazards such as cess-pits, cow houses and dust bins as well as the more usual information recorded by the OS. Most of these plans remain unpublished, and though some are in local record offices, others are still with borough engineers and the like, and a few are feared lost.

In 1855 1:500 was adopted as the standard urban scale, and by 1895 every town of sufficient size had been mapped at this scale. Between 1870 and 1908

83

a few towns were revised at 1:500, but most were revised at only 1:2500. Copies of the revisions often have to be sought in local collections.

   2.   The 1:2500. This was the standard scale for rural mapping from 1853 onwards, except for larger moorland areas, which were only mapped at six-inch. The sheet layout and the survey and revision system were arranged by counties. Priority was given to those parts of northern Britain which had not hitherto been mapped at any scale by the OS, and so the mapping of northern England and lowland Scotland precedes that of southern Britain. For those areas surveyed between 1853 and the late 1870s 'area books' were published, with land use information. From *circa* 1879 onwards the depiction of land-use was effectively confined to varieties of uncultivated land and woodland. The first edition was completed in 1895, and a second edition in 1914. Between 1907 and 1922 about half of England and Wales, but a much smaller proportion of Scotland, was published in a *de facto* third edition (usually described on the maps as 'Edition of'). After 1922 revision by whole counties was replaced by revision of small blocks of sheets covering developing areas, although the county sheet lines were retained.
   Two other versions of the 1:2500 may be noted here. Between *circa* 1870 and 1890 a few groups of 1:2500 sheets were revised before the general revision began in 1891. These include some around London, and some of areas mapped (for military reasons) in the early 1860s before the remainder of the country had been started. Copies of these must be sought in local collections. In 1911-12 extensive revision of urban areas was carried out in conjunction with Land Valuation (the 'Lloyd George Domesday', see Short Guide 36). Most of these sheets were apparently not published, but there is a nearly complete set in the Public Record Office (classes IR 121-135), and some local record offices have substantial holdings.
   From 1911 onwards 1:1250 photo-enlargements of the 1:2500 were produced, initially for Land Valuation purposes. These enlargements are sometimes found in local collections; they contain no more information than is to be found in the parent maps.

   3.   The six-inch. This was the standard scale for all rural areas from 1841 to 1853, when it was displaced as the largest scale for rural mapping by the 1:2500. Edinburghshire, Fife, Haddingtonshire, Kinross, Kirkcudbrightshire, Lancashire, Lewis, Wigtownshire and Yorkshire were published at this scale at this time. After 1853 the six-inch continued to be the largest scale for moorland areas (in some remote parts of Scotland this could include settlements), and elsewhere it was published as a derivative of the 1:2500. Two exceptions to this are (1) there is no six-inch equivalent to the 1911-12 Land Valuation revision and (2) in 1938-39 a 'Special Emergency Edition' was produced, which was intended to show the basics of new roads and building development, and which is extremely useful as a guide to urbanisation on the eve of World War II for all settlements of over about 2500 population. Unfortunately copies of the Special Emergency Edition are hard to find and it is usually necessary to resort either to the 'Provisional Edition' of the six-inch, published from 1943 onwards (where not later revised), or to the 1:25,000 series GSGS 3906, which was produced in 1940-41 by direct photo-reduction from the latest available six-inch mapping.

4.   The one-inch. The most familiar of OS mapping to the public, it is also the most difficult to generalise about. For that part of Britain south of a line from Preston to Hull the one-inch was the earliest OS mapping to be published. It was based on surveys made between 1784 and 1840, mostly at the two-inch (1:31,680) scale, but including some at the three-inch (1:21,120) and six-inch scales. The published map is generally known as the 'Old Series'. The progress of survey and publication was roughly south-north. Over much of the midlands and Wales the two-inch surveys were extensively revised before publication, so that the published mapping is preceded by unpublished manuscript mapping. The facsimile publication in volume form by Harry Margary is derived from originals in this early state. In the 1830s and 1840s a few sheets were wholly revised; otherwise revision was confined to the addition of railways, and some piecemeal additions, mostly to urban areas. The 'first editions' published by David and Charles are all based on these later partially revised states, and are of limited use as historical sources.

North of the Preston-Hull line the early one-inch sheets were generalised reductions from the six-inch and larger scale surveys of 1840 onwards, and are thus of far less interest than the earlier Old Series mapping. The mapping of southern Britain at 1:2500 from 1859 onwards was complemented by the replacement of the Old Series by the New Series, reduced from the six-inch and larger-scale mapping.

From 1893 onwards the one-inch was revised independently of the larger scales, and as a result it can provide an intermediate stage between generations of the 1:2500 and six-inch. These intermediate generations are the revisions of 1893-98 (known as the 'revised New Series' in England and Wales), 1901-12 ('Third Edition') and 1912-30, ('Popular Edition'); a Fifth Edition, revised 1928-40, was abandoned after it had covered most of southern England.

USES

Old Ordnance Survey Maps may be used for studying changes in field boundaries, the general shape of buildings, public boundaries, communications, and, to a certain extent, land-use and vegetation, both as a 'snapshot' at the time of survey or revision, and, by comparison with other maps, as part of a continuing process over time. Landscape changes can be dated approximately by interpolation. For practical purposes, Ordnance Survey maps may be taken as an authoritative statement on public boundaries and administrative names current at the time the map was made, and for other purposes OS maps have the status of *prima facie* evidence in courts of law. They are also useful as records of place names, though, particularly on the first editions of the six-inch and larger-scale maps, the orthography of some Scottish and Welsh placenames is not completely reliable and should be cross-checked against other sources where possible.

LOCATION

There is unfortunately no reliable survey of the location of Ordnance Survey maps. Local record offices and the local studies sections of public libraries usually have some six-inch and larger-scale coverage, but this can vary from fairly complete coverage of a county in all editions to incomplete coverage by a single edition (or composite of editions) of the six-inch and 1:2500. The most complete collection of Ordnance Survey maps is that of the British Library Map Library (access to which for *bona fide* users is much easier than it is to the main reading-rooms of the BL), and other extensive collections are held by the other legal deposit libraries.

BIBLIOGRAPHY

Andrews, J H, *History in the Ordnance map: an introduction for Irish readers* (1974), reprinted Kerry, David Archer, (1993). This can also be read with profit by British users.

Harley, J B, 'The Ordnance Survey and land-use mapping' *Historical Geography Research Series* no.2, Norwich, Geo Books, (1979). A most useful introduction to its subject, covering 1855-1918, and to date the most detailed published study of an aspect of OS mapping.

Harley, J B and Walters, Gwyn, 'Welsh orthography and Ordnance Survey mapping, 1820-1905'; *Archaeologia Cambrensis*, CXXXI (1982), 98-135. This is a useful guide to an aspect of the virtues and limitations of OS maps as records of place names.

Oliver, Richard, *Ordnance Survey maps: a concise guide for historians*, (London, Charles Close Society, 1993). This includes details of what scales were published for what localities at what times, notes on the depiction of details on OS maps, a list of abbreviations and a select bibliography.

Ordnance Survey of England and Wales: indexes to the 1/2500 and 6-inch, (c.1905), Kerry, David Archer, (1991).

Ordnance Survey of Scotland: indexes to the 1/2500 and 6 -inch, (c.1907), Kerry, David Archer, (1993).

These volumes are extremely useful both to show the sheet layouts of these maps, and to indicate the extent of areas mapped at the 6-inch scale but not at the 1:2500.

41
Aerial Photography for Archaeology

Bob Bewley

Aerial photography for archaeological purposes began in the 1920s with the work of O.G.S. Crawford in England and in a variety of places throughout Europe and the Middle East.

As a result of over 90 years of photography a large amount of expertise and archaeological research has developed in the use of aerial photographs for archaeological and historical purposes. A research group was formed in 1980 (the Aerial Archaeology Research Group) initially with a British interest but since 1990, with the opening up of central and eastern Europe, it has become international in its membership.

WHAT ARE AERIAL PHOTOGRAPHS?

There are two sorts of aerial photographs, verticals and obliques: both are useful for historical and archaeological research. Vertical aerial photographs are mostly commercial surveys or county census surveys; they are rarely taken for specifically archaeological purposes. One collection of historic vertical photographs, taken by the RAF between 1945 and 1948 contains invaluable information of the British landscape as it was immediately after the Second World War. This collection, which consists of over 5 million photographs is available for consultation in England, Scotland and Wales (see below for addresses of the three Royal Commissions). Vertical photographs, if taken in stereoscopic pairs, allow for the closer examination with the use of a stereoscope, and therefore can provide for more accurate interpretations (the same is true for obliques, but see below). For vertical photography a high-quality camera, mounted in an aircraft, is an essential requirement.

Oblique aerial photographs, sometimes referred to as specialist archaeological photographs, are taken with medium format and 35 mm cameras from an open window in a light aircraft. This technique has been used for many years and there are a number of collections available for consultation throughout Britain (see NAPLIB directory reference below). The oblique view, which can be captured in stereoscopic pairs, has the advantage over a vertical in that it can highlight the archaeological features by obtaining the optimum angle of light. The archaeological features are either earthworks, cropmarks, soilmarks or parchmarks. Standing buildings are also regularly photographed; obtaining the best angle of view is also critical if these sites are to be shown to their best advantage, either for illustrative reasons or to show the site in its historical context.

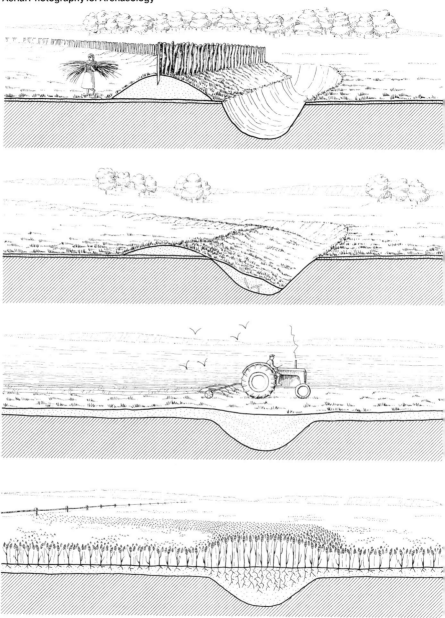

Representation of the way in which sites which originally had a ditch, bank and palisade, perhaps for defence, silt up, become levelled and are ultimately revealed as cropmarks. *West Yorkshire Archaeology Service*

WHAT DO AERIAL PHOTOGRAPHS SHOW?

On all aerial photographs there are historical and archaeological features and considerable skill is required in their interpretation. These features may be relatively modern (buildings, urban areas, field boundaries, drainage patterns, military installations) or more ancient (for example prehistoric sites, Roman forts and camps, medieval earthworks etc.).

Apart from existing upstanding features there are also buried remains which are made visible either as cropmarks or soilmarks (see representation, left). Cropmarks and soilmarks are formed when a ditch (which has been dug for protection or drainage) has filled up, and the ditch-fill contains more water and more nutrients than the surrounding soil. The crop above the ditch will grow taller and ripen later than the surrounding crop; when this is viewed from the air it usually shows as a darker (greener) mark in the field. If the field is surveyed from the air, when ploughed, the ditch (or any other feature, wall etc) may show as a differentially coloured mark. The dryer the summer season (i.e. the growing season) the greater the probability that cropmarks will be visible. In exceptionally dry years it is also possible to record sites in parched grass; walls and earthen banks are commonly visible but ditches can also be seen when parching occurs.

WHO TAKES THE AERIAL PHOTOGRAPHS?

In Britain the main programmes of flying are carried out by the three Royal Commissions and a network of regional flyers which they coordinate and assist with funds (often with other funding bodies). The photographs from these flying programmes are stored in the appropriate national libraries as well as local collections. There are other national collections and perhaps the most important is the Cambridge University Collection of Aerial Photographs (address below) which has been flying and surveying for archaeological sites since 1945, taking both oblique and vertical photographs.

WHO USES AERIAL PHOTOGRAPHS?

For archaeological and historical purposes aerial photographs or maps derived from them are used on a daily basis. All the county archaeological Sites and Monuments Records have access to photographs and maps created from a variety of sources. The national bodies, especially the three Royal Commissions for England, Scotland and Wales have national programmes for mapping the whole country based on aerial photographs. England's National Mapping Programme aims to interpret, map and make records of all the archaeological sites, seen on aerial photographs; the mapping scale is 1:10,000 and the maps are available for use in the National Monuments Record Centre, Swindon. The maps and the collections of photographs are an important resource for all archaeologists and historians, especially landscape historians. The results of the mapping programme provide a reliable national framework for future research into the understanding of the development of the English landscape. For each project area there has been at least a 45 % increase in records for hitherto unknown sites and this

SP 4003/24   SP401035 03-JUL-90   NMR 4694/53

Stanalake, Oxfordshire. The village (top) represents the living but historic environments which can be recorded from the air. However, the earthworks (top centre) represent the former extent of a shrunken medieval village. The black lines of cropmarks (centre) reveal buried ditches of settlements and burials from the Roman and prehistoric periods. The gravel pits (bottom) are testament to the 20th century's destruction of large areas of river gravel.
RHCME Crown Copyright. SP 4003/24. NMR 4694/53. Date: 3 July 1990.

is only from the information derived from aerial photographs. When the results from aerial photography are combined with fieldwork there is an even greater increase in information and understanding.

The maps and database are used by university research workers, but the major users are those archaeologists involved with development and planning control work. Evaluations of sites and areas prior to any development have become standard practice (especially through the Policy and Planning Guidance Note 16); interpretative maps and records derived from these aerial photographs are the quickest and most effective method of producing these evaluations. English Heritage also makes significant use of the information from England's National Mapping Programme especially for its Monuments Protection Programme, which aims to increase the number of sites under statutory protection.

The national historic collections have also been widely used by engineers, looking for changes in land use, and solicitors and lawyers in boundary disputes.

WHERE ARE THE COLLECTIONS AND LIBRARIES?

There are three main groups of collections; private, county based and national. The NAPLIB directory (see below) lists many of the collections which are available for consultation, including those held by private individuals. Many county councils hold collections of verticals (and some obliques) mainly those taken for the census surveys taken every ten years. The main national collections for archaeological and historical research are those held by the three Royal Commissions and the Cambridge collection. Other national agencies such as the OS, MAFF, English Nature and the Environment Agency all commission vertical surveys and have varying degrees of access. Similarly, the commercial companies (e.g. Aerofilms) have collections which are accessible at certain times.

SELECT BIBLIOGRAPHY

Bewley R.H. 'Aerial Photography for Archaeology' in Hunter J. and Ralston I. *Archaeological Resource Management in the UK*, pp 197 - 204. (Alan Sutton, 1993)

Crawford O. G. S. *Air survey and Archaeology* Ordnance Survey Professional papers, new series 7 (Ordnance Survey, 1928)

Crawford O.G.S & Keiller A. *Wessex from the Air* (Oxford University Press, 1928)

Deuel L. *Flights into Yesterday* (MacDonald, New York, 1969)

Palmer R. *Danebury: an Aerial Photographic Interpretation of its Environs* (RCHME, Supplementary Series No. 6, 1984)

Palmer R and Cox C. *The Uses of Aerial Photography in Archaeological Evaluations* IFA Technical Paper No. 12. (IFA, 1993)

Poidebard A. *La Trace De Rome dans le Desert de Syrie* Bibliotheque Archeologique et Historique Tome XVIII. (Paul Geuthner, Paris, 1934)

Riley D.N. *Aerial Archaeology in Britain* (Shire Publications, 1996)

Riley D.N. *Air Photography and Archaeology* (Duckworth, 1987)

RCHME *A Matter of Time* (HMSO, 1960)

St Joseph J.K.S *Uses of Air Photography* (John Baker, 1966)

Wilson D.R. *Air Photo Interpretation for Archaeologists* (Batsford, 1982)

CONTACT ADDRESSES

AARG: Aerial Archaeology Research Group. This group meets annually to discuss the techniques, discoveries, and all matters concerning aerial photography for archaeology. It has no permanent address as its Officers rotate; for further information write to one of the Royal Commission addresses below.

CUCAP: The Mond Building, Free School Lane, Cambridge, CB2 3RF. Tel: 01223 334578 The Collection may be visited by members of the public during normal office hours. Photographs cannot be borrowed but prints can be purchased; orders ordinarily take about a month. Prices depend on print size from £3.06 for a 5" x 5" black and white to £11.75 for 9"x 9" colour positives. Copyright is retained by the University or the Crown.

NAPLIB: National Association of Aerial Photographic Libraries. (c/o The Curator, CUCAP)

RCHME: The Royal Commission of the Historical Monuments of England. NMRC, Great Western Village, Kemble Drive, Swindon, SN2 2GZ. The national body for survey and record in England.

NMR: National Monuments Record: Air Photographs. RCHME, Great Western Village, Kemble Drive, Swindon, SN2 2NG. Tel: 01793 414700. This is a branch of the National Monuments Record for England. Photographs can be consulted by prior arrangement. An express service can be provided for urgent requests (costs and details from the above address).

RCHAMW: The Royal Commission on the Ancient and Historical Monuments of Wales. Crown Buildings, Plas Crug, Aberystwyth, Dyfed, SY23 2HP. The national body of survey and record for Wales.

RCHAMS: The Royal Commission on the Ancient and Historical Monuments of Scotland. John Sinclair House, 16 Bemard Terrace, Edinburgh, EH8 9NX. The national body of survey and record for Scotland.

Canal & Railway Plans
David Smith

ORIGIN

Plans of canals and railways accompanied schemes as they came into being and their subsequent operation. Their antecedents are the scarce plans of river improvements and waggonways (or tramways, dramroads or mineral lines) that preceded the canals and railways. From 1793 private canal or waterworks' bills submitted to Parliament, involving new works or compulsory acquisition of land, had to be accompanied by a plan of the proposed works. This requirement was extended to railway bills from 1803. In 1836 elaborate new procedures were introduced for railway bills.

For promoters to choose the most suitable route a feasibility survey was made and levels taken, although this rarely recorded much topographical detail. Once Parliamentary sanction was granted, detailed engineering plans were prepared for construction and maintenance, often by superimposing engineering details onto existing Ordnance and Tithe Survey maps. When the scheme came into operation maps were prepared by the companies to facilitate efficient working.

The most reliable railway network maps are those produced on a semi-official basis by employees of the Railway Clearing House, notably Zachary Macaulay and, especially, John Airey, and later by the House itself. Small-scale maps of lines or networks illustrated a scheme's prospectus, publicity, propaganda, timetables, guides and handbooks. Network and regional maps accompanied contemporary accounts and histories and were issued commercially in sheets, atlases, topographies and as wall maps. John Cary, the renowned nineteenth century mapmaker, produced an atlas of canal plans, and railway maps were published from the 1850s by the *Weekly Dispatch* and later Cassell & Co. Popular interest was further satisfied by the appearance of maps in periodicals such as the *Gentleman's Magazine.*

LOCATION

Although canal and railway plans will be found in virtually all archives, often hidden in non-transport categories, a number of locations stand out as being of primary importance. Surviving Parliamentary plans and associated documents, whether deposited with private bills or accompanying public bills, can be consulted at the House of Lords Record Office. Those deposited locally are generally now in County Record Offices or other regional/local archives. The Public Record Office holds extensive records of both official bodies and individual companies; note that plans may reside in the records of the Treasury, Home Office, War Office, Land Revenue Office, Forestry Commission, Harbour departments, Commissioners of Works, Duchy of Lancaster, and other records, particularly legal, not specifically designated as maps. Similarly, transport plans, particularly of railways, form a substantial group in the Scottish Record Office. London transport records are found in the London Metropolitan Archives (formerly known as the Greater London Record Office). University and college libraries sometimes house important records, notably the O'Dell Collection in Aberdeen University Library and the maps and plans from St Enoch's station in Glasgow which are held in Paisley College Library. The acquisition of the Clinker and Garnett collections and the Transport Trust Library has made Brunel University Library a premier centre for the study of railway history. The National Railway Museum holds some 300 plans; the British Waterways Archive estimates its collection as some 8,000 maps, plans and drawings; and the Institution of Civil Engineers has 'one of the world's leading civil engineering collections'. Other significant plan collections are those in Bolton Archive Service and Cheshire Record Office. The Railway and Canal Historical Society maintains an index, arranged by company, of some 140,000 cards identifying document locations.

FORMAT

Small-scale maps of a route prepared for prospectuses, atlases, timetables, handbooks, guides, publicity and periodicals, usually superimposed the line of route onto a landscape of or copied from an earlier map. However, the larger-scale, more accurate, and therefore more useful and reliable, transport maps tend to delineate only the line of route and the land either side, extending to a distance of about 1/4 mile and portraying the full range of landscape features in detail. Each land plot to be acquired was numbered to correspond with its description in the Book of Reference. Additional features found on or accompanying strip maps include larger–scale insets of towns or important estates, distance tables, schedules of estimated costs, tidal ranges, population details, competitive mileages by rival routes, notes of potential freight, and plans and drawings of associated infrastructure such as bridges, viaducts and aqueducts, stations and tunnels. Longitudinal sections showing the level of the ground in relation to the height or depth of the works were frequently included with plans from 1795, being required for railways from 1836 at specified scales. Also from 1836 small-scale maps showing the general direction of railway lines were required but many have failed to survive. Scales of deposited plans vary enormously, often being much larger than those legally required. Standing Orders progressively increased required scales over the years, notably for railway plans which from 1836 had a minimum scale requirement of 4 inches to the mile with built-up areas to be much enlarged, particularly to delineate the impact of terminus construction.

In addition to covering full routes when proposals were first submitted to Parliament, plans were also required when a branch, extension or doubling was added, a route altered, and even for minor alterations such as modifications to individual locks or sections of line. Canals were surveyed again in the event of takeover by a competing railway company anxious to utilise the same route. In addition to plans originally deposited there may well also be amended plans with alterations, agreed during the committee proceedings as proposals moved from

Commons to Lords, initialled by the chairman. Thus a family of plans with progressive modifications may illustrate the development of a scheme. From 1838 duplicate plans had to be deposited locally, although in practice this had often been done before, and many will now be found in local record offices.

Early deposited plans are manuscript drawings, either plain or coloured, on paper or parchment. From 1795 it was required that they should be engraved and printed. However once the appropriate large-scale Ordnance Survey sheets became available it was sufficient to superimpose proposals onto the Ordnance's accurate landscape.

USES AND INTERPRETATION

In addition to their obvious value in depicting the details of canal and railway schemes, large-scale strip maps also offer a detailed view of the immediate landscape. They may well be the most accurate and informative contemporary maps available, being particularly important when they pre-date large-scale Ordnance Survey mapping or fall between Ordnance editions. Since plans presented to Parliament were subject to the scrutiny of opponents and formed the basis of legislation, they generally represent relatively accurate records although some railway mapping, particularly during periods of 'mania', was rushed by incompetent, inexperienced surveyors. Although many proposed schemes never reached construction their plans nevertheless illuminate proposals and record the contemporary landscape.

The route ownership, co-ownership, through-running facilities and other railway information portrayed by Airey and the Railway Clearing House particularly is of primary importance and was regularly revised. However it was simply superimposed on the Ordnance Survey's base maps.

Most promotional maps were copied from existing small-scale maps by fairly careless engraving or lithography because accuracy was unimportant. Hence, although valuable as background to a project, their topographical evidence and even the line of route are unreliable. General network maps frequently confused projected with constructed schemes and portrayed those never built. The most reliable are those published by George Bradshaw and the engineers themselves, and those prepared for official purposes.

Regional, county and environs' maps superimposing a network onto an existing landscape, frequently issued as pocket travelling maps, should not be trusted despite their designation as 'canal' or 'railway' maps. Similarly, transport features on large-scale and other county maps are unreliable. On general maps only the Ordnance Survey's representation of canals and railways is above suspicion.

ANCILLARY RECORDS

Documents associated with canal and railway plans are: (i) those necessary for understanding plans presented to Parliament; (ii) those related to the Parliamentary process containing further plans; (iii) those required to accompany plans presented to Parliament but not directly linked to them; (iv) those containing or accompanying plans produced by engineers or companies; (v) those accompanying plans produced for prospective shareholders, actual shareholders and travellers, and to satisfy popular interest.

(i) The indispensable document for the interpretation of deposited plans is the Book of Reference. From 1794 for canals and 1803 for railways, plans presented to Parliament had to be accompanied by a Book which identified the numbered plots shown on the plan by owner or reputed owner, occupier and lessee (at least from 1838). Land use was identified with general descriptions of property.

(ii) Among the mass of documents generated in gaining Parliamentary approval and in subsequent enquiry and legislation, some required their own explanatory maps and plans. These might accompany the carefully documented reports of Select Committees or appear in their minutes of evidence. Others illustrated records, minutes, proceedings, reports, evidence and correspondence produced by enquiry and the legislative process, as they might enquiries and petitions made to Parliament. Plans accompanied such official investigations as the *Returns and Plans of Iron Bridges* (1847). Particularly important is the 12-volume *Report of the Royal Commission on the Canals and Inland Navigations of the United Kingdom* (1906-11) with its excellent maps. From 1853 demolition statements (or 'working class statements' or 'rehousing statements'), frequently illustrated by large-scale plans, described persons and property involved in significant building clearance in 'working class' areas. Maps and plans also appear in the judicial records of transport cases heard by the House of Lords in its role as the highest court of appeal.

(iii) Passage of a proposal through Parliament also produced a wide range of documents relating to the project but not specifically to deposited plans. These were not generally illustrated by maps. However these documents such as Consents Lists, Subscription Contracts, and Estimates, required from various dates, illuminate aspects of schemes which their plans cannot, providing a wider perspective.

(iv) The records of engineers and companies contain numerous plans and related documents such as specifications, estimates, contracts, agreements and correspondence.

(v) Maps issued with the prospectus for a scheme or broadsheets and pamphlets attacking or supporting it must be interpreted in the light of their accompanying propaganda. Similarly maps in popular periodicals often illustrated accompanying explanatory articles.

BIBLIOGRAPHY

Some record offices, libraries, local history societies and other organisations produce listings of their transport map collections, particularly relating to railways.

Bond, Maurice, *Guide to the Records of Parliament* (1971), pp79-80, 85-86, 89-90

Brunel University Library, *Railway Maps and the Railway Clearing House. The David Garnett Collection in Brunel University Library* (1986) contains articles by David Garnett and others, and also a full bibliography of articles on railway maps by David Garnett published in the *Journal of the Railway and Canal Historical Society*, *The Map Collector* and elsewhere between 1959 and 1984. See also the catalogue to the exhibition (1986). A catalogue of David Garnett's collection is in preparation for publication.

Cary, John, *Inland Navigation; or Select Plans of the Several Navigable Canals throughout Great Britain* (in parts, 1795-1808)

Fowkes, E H, *Railway History and the Local Historian* (East Yorkshire Local History Society 1963)

Hadfield, Charles, 'Sources for the history of British canals', *Journal of Transport History*, vol 2, 1955-56, pp 80-89. The *Journal* has published other articles which refer to sources for canal and railway maps and ancillary records, see: Bond, M, vol 4, 1959-60, pp37-52; Dyos, H J, vol 2, 1955-56, pp11-21, 90-100, and vol 3, 1957-58, pp23-30; Johnson, L C, vol 1, 1953-54, pp82-96; Simmons, J, vol 1, 1953-54, pp155-169; Wardle, D B, vol 2, 1955-56, pp214-34. See also: Cobb, H S, in *Archives*, vol 9, 1969, pp73-79, and Robbins, M, in *Railway Magazine*, vol 99, 1953, pp228-229, 276. Innumerable works cover transport plans incidentally in the study of transport history, particularly those on canals by Charles Hadfield.

Hampshire Archivists' Group, *Transport in Hampshire and the Isle of Wight. A Guide to the Records*, (Publication no 2, 1973)

Harley, J B, *Maps for the Local Historian. A Guide to the British Sources* (Standing Conference for Local History, 1977), pp40-42, 45-50

Hindle, Paul, *Maps for Local History* (1988), pp107-118

Moir, D G (ed) *The Early Maps of Scotland to 1850* (Edinburgh, 1983), vol 2, pp57-122

Public Record Office, 'Records relating to Railways' (*Records Information* no 32, 1990)

Skempton, A W, *Early Printed Reports and Maps (1665-1850) in the Library of the Institution of Civil Engineers* (1977)

Skempton, A W, *British Civil Engineering 1640-1840: A Bibliography of Contemporary Printed Reports, Plans and Books* (1987)

Smith, David, *Victorian Maps of the British Isles* (1985), pp82-3, 91-103

Smith, David, *Maps and Plans for the Local Historian and Collector* (1988), pp35, 112-113, 123-134

Smith, David, *British Urban Mapping of Waterways, Canals and Docks* (forthcoming)

Smith, David, *The Railway Mapping of British Towns* (forthcoming)

Torrens, H S, 'Early maps of the Somersetshire Coal Canal', *Cartographic Journal*, vol 11 no 1, 1974, pp45-47) For further discussion see: Eyles, J M, (pp.47-48) and Torrens, S, (p.49), vol.12, no.1, (1975).

Fire Insurance Plans
Peter A Neaverson

ORIGIN

During the later part of the eighteenth century insurance underwriters, in order to assess fire risk premiums, required information not only on the physical structure of the building to be insured but also details of its location within a built-up area. In particular, a knowledge of the spatial relationship of the building to their other policyholders' property was essential in order to limit the insurance company's liabilities and losses as a result of a major fire outbreak. Such specialised plans

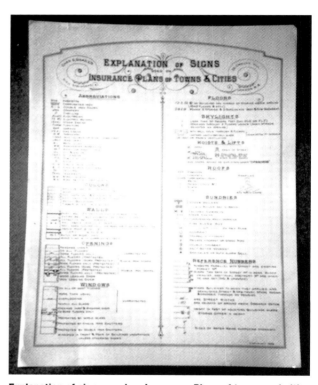

Explanation of signs used on Insurance Plans of towns and cities

were first produced by the insurance companies themselves for their exclusive use and examples survive of Sun Insurance Office and Phoenix Assurance Company plans dating from the 1780s. In 1857 the Phoenix company surveyor, James Loveday, published his 'Waterside Surveys' for the north and south banks of the River Thames in London; these were made available to some 28 subscribers, including rival insurance companies.

The most comprehensive range of Fire Insurance Plans produced in a standard format were those of Charles E Goad (1848-1910) and his company. Goad, an Englishman by birth, went to Canada first as a railway engineer; he

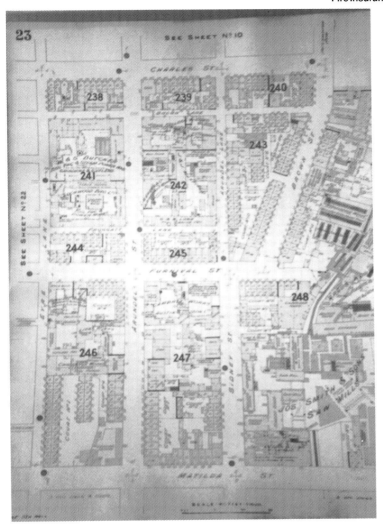

Sheffield sheet 22 January 1963 (20th revision)

produced his first plan in 1875 of Leavis in Quebec. He emulated the work of the American D A Sanborn Company, which had in 1869 foreseen the need for such plans for the largely timber-built North American towns. British fire insurance companies covered this risk market and were faced with large claims following several major city fires there between 1860 and1910. Goad returned to London in 1885 and established a British branch, producing his first series of detailed plans for London in 1886. Within ten years 53 series of plans had been produced

The Sheffield key plan revised to January 1963 (20th revision)

for central districts of major urban areas and for major commercial and industrial districts where particular concerns were warehousing and transport termini for canals, ports and railways. In all, some 126 series of the plans were produced, including 12 for which outline surveys only were made; presumably enough subscribers were not found to justify full surveys in those places. Subscribers leased a key plan with street index for the area: these indicated those blocks for which detailed plans were supplied. Revisions of detailed plans were carried out, sometimes annually or biennially, on an average of between five and six years; the revisions could consist of additional new plans or paste-on overlays for rebuilt blocks of property. The service was continued until 1970, and lapsed subscribers should have returned their plans to the Goad company. Chas E Goad Ltd now publish plans for over 1000 shopping centres in the major conurbations, showing names and trades of occupants.

LOCATION AND FORMAT OF RECORDS

Early Fire Insurance Plans are held at the Guildhall Library in London whilst some remain in the hands of insurance companies. The Goad plans are more widely spread but even so were originally limited to private subscribers. The British Museum holds a comprehensive collection and many are held in local record offices and university map collections. Undoubtedly many survive in other hands. For example in the case of the Leicester series, published from 1892 to 1961, there were 47 subscribers, including 42 insurance companies, the Corporation of Leicester and one estate agent. Chas E Goad Ltd also offer for sale their remainder stock of plans. Their address is 8 Salisbury Square, Hatfield, Hertfordshire, AL9 5AD.

The areas of the British Isles for which detailed plans have been produced are as follows. The dates shown refer to the original publication and the last revision:

Bath	1902-58	Kidderminster	1897-1943
Batley	1893-1958	Kings Lynn	1909-33
Belfast	1887-1961	Leeds	1886-1971
Birmingham	1889-1965	Leicester	1892-1961
Bradford	1886-1961	Leith	1892-1960
Brighton	1898-1952	Limerick	1897-1961
Bristol	1887-1961	Lincoln	1902-33
Campbeltown	1898-1909	Liverpool	1888-1969
Canterbury	1912-43	London	1886-1970
Cardiff	1909-61	Marylebone	1934
Chatham	1912-29	Shoreditch	1935
Chelmsford	1909-54	Londonderry	1899-1961
Colchester	1899-1954	Long Eaton	1908-29
Cork	1897-1961	Luton	1895-1958
Coventry	1897-1959	Maidstone	1912-43
Dewsbury	1892-1928	Manchester	1888-1970
Dover	1905-29	Newcastle	1887-1962
Dublin	1893-1961	Newport, Mon	1888-1961
Dundee	1887-1961	Northampton	1899-1956
Edinburgh	1892-1960	Norwich	1894-1955
Exeter	1888-1962	Nottingham	1886-1962
Glasgow	1887-1970	Paisley	1888-1956
Gloucester	1891-1955	Plymouth	1891-1962
Goole	1896-1959	Reading	1895-1958

Greenock	1888-1960	Sheffield	1896-1963
Grimsby	1896-1959	Southampton	1893-1959
Halifax	1887-1962	Sunderland	1894-1962
Huddersfield	1887-1962	Swansea	1888-1961
Hull	1886-1962	Thames Valley	1907-8
Ipswich	1899-1958	Yarmouth	1899-1946

Birkenhead and Wallasey are included with Liverpool, and Trafford with Manchester. In the Lower Thames Valley series there are plans of Barking, Charlton, Crayford and Dartford, Dagenham, Erith, Gravesend, Grays and Thurrock, Northfleet, Purfleet, Rainham and Woolwich. The Upper Thames Valley series covers Brentford and Kew Bridge, Chiswick, Isleworth, Kingston upon Thames, Mortlake and Barnes, Putney and Wandsworth, Richmond, Teddington and Twickenham.

Preliminary key plans were made for the following towns:

Bedford	1900	Loughborough	1900
Boston	1900	Lowestoft	1899
Bury St Edmunds	1900	Margate	1900
Cambridge	1900	Peterborough	1900
Croydon	1900	Ramsgate	1900
Folkestone	1900	Wellingborough	1900
Guildford	1900		

The plans were produced in a range of scales, key plans 200, 300, 400, 500 or 600ft to l" and detail plans 40 or 80ft to l". All sheets are of a standard size 20 $^3/_4$ inches by 25 inches and are dated and numbered. The type of building material is indicated by means of colour shading. Water main sizes and fire hydrants are shown, important information for the fire insurance underwriter. Dimensions of buildings, number of storeys, basement depths (if any) and street numbers and street widths are also included. In the case of the larger commercial and industrial buildings, the name and occupation of the occupier are given. The methods of heating and lighting are also shown together with any power sources such as steam or gas engines or electric motors. Fire extinguishing equipment is also indicated. A comprehensive key to the symbols employed is provided.

Specialised plans prepared include:

Leeds Carriers	1896-1971
Liverpool Mercantile Warehouses	1885
Manchester Carriers	1891-1970
River Tyne Docks	1894-1927
Hartlepool Docks	1894-1952

These special plans include even more detail with full descriptions, plans, sections and isometric drawings of large buildings such as warehouses and granaries. The Leeds plan shows the canal and railway network and warehouses within a 17 mile radius of the city whilst that for Manchester covers a larger region up to 30 miles radius. The Dock plans show port and riverside installations, warehouses and railways.

USES OF THE RECORDS

The detailed plans, revised at more frequent intervals than the large scale Ordnance Survey maps, enable an accurate picture of growth and development to be constructed for selected urban areas. The plans are unique in showing vertical extensions of buildings, with numbers and heights of storeys and basement depths. The information thereon can be supplemented by data from trade directories, rate books, census returns, local authority building plans, old photographs and other records. Successive editions of the plans show in some cases several phases of redevelopment, including demolition of housing for industrial development and even rebuilding after war damage. The plans, with their detail of building structures, will be of use to the architectural historian. The urban archaeologist will be able to ascertain the presence and depth of cellars and assess their possible destruction of underground archaeology. The industrial archaeologist is provided with much information concerning local industry, including types of machinery and power sources employed. The urban historian, will, for the areas for which the plans are published, be able to study the growth of towns and cities, the decay of inner areas, the spread of suburbia and working class housing. The economic geographer, business and economic historians also have a detailed resource to enable them to study the development and movement of industry and commerce within the areas covered. The transport historian is provided with information concerning installations and warehouses on the specialist plans which is probably nowhere else as easily accessible.

BIBLIOGRAPHY

Aspinall, Peter J, 'The use of nineteenth century insurance plans for the urban historian' *The Local Historian*, Vol 11, No 6, 1975, pp342-9. [This article contains a list of those Goad plans then held in The Map Collection at the British Musuem.]

Cockerell, H A L and Green, E, *The British Insurance Business 1547-1970: An Introduction and Guide to Historical Research in the United Kingdom* (1976)

Hindle, Brian Paul, *Maps for Local History* (1988)

Hyde, R N, 'Notes on a collection of London Insurance Surveys, 1794-1807 *Journal of Society of Archivists*, 4, 1970-3 pp327-9; 'More early Insurance Surveys come to light' *Journal of Society of Archivists*, 4, 1970-3, p523

Rowley, Gwyn, *British Fire Insurance Plans* (Old Hatfield, 1984)

44
School Log Books
Pamela Horn

(A) LOG BOOK OF ST. CLEMENT'S BOYS' SCHOOL, LIVERPOOL, AT LIVERPOOL RECORD OFFICE, 1862

Oct 2nd The testing of the 2nd Class to ascertain their fitness for Examination by HM Inspector, was not satisfactory in its results. The other divisions of the school were very satisfactory. School rather noisy during the day.

Oct 6th The teachers, on the whole, were attentive to their classes, although some bad blots were found in the writing books of the 1st class and 3rd Section. Arithmetic not satisfactory in 1st Class in the Morning, but very satisfactory throughout the school in the Afternoon.

Oct 8th John McDonald [stipendiary monitor] disobedient in playing with the pupils about the premises — thus encouraging them to loiter about the building after having been forbidden to do so. Behaviour and attention of the rest very good.

(B) LOG BOOK OF BRADFORD PARISH CHURCH NATIONAL [I.E. ANGLICAN] BOYS' SCHOOL, 19D75/9/3 IN BRADFORD DISTRICT ARCHIVES, 1863

Jany 6 A few scholars have given notice to leave rather than pay the extra penny for school pence.

Jany 7 I have had occasion to reprove one of my teachers today for striking one of the scholars.

Jany 9 Issued Circulars to Mill Masters & Parents, announcing the increase of payment, in consequence of the New Code & Regulations.

Jany 14 Rouse's mill-hands have left this School in consequence of the increase of payments.

Jany 15 It is rumoured that two or three other Mills have said their children will be taken away from this School.

Jany 16 Received notice that the above rumour is false.

Jany 19 Rouse's mill children have returned.

Jany 22 The Sub-Inspector of Factories called today.

Feb 2 A lecture delivered on Phrenology by a travelling lecturer.

Feb 11 School closed at 3.30 to let the Scholars go to a Panorama.

(C) LOG BOOK OF STEEPLE ASTON NATIONAL SCHOOL, OXFORDSHIRE, T/SL.5(I) IN OXFORDSHIRE ARCHIVES, 1863

Sept 14 School reopened after harvest holidays. Gleaning not finished: school thin in consequence, only 28 present.

Sept 18 Very small school the whole week. Children employed gleaning & getting up potatoes.

Sept 21 31 present. Rousham and Middle Aston children absent on account of Scarlet Fever being in the village. Several children still at harvest work. Punished G Durran & W Barret for neglect of lessons.

Sept 23 Warned the school against stone threwing [sic] & cruelty to animals.

ORIGIN
School log books were first introduced late in 1862 as part of a general move by the government to promote efficiency, economy and accountability in elementary education. Under the Education Department's regulatory Revised Code of that year all elementary schools open to public inspection — and thus eligible for state grants — had to maintain a regular record of activities. Those schools without a certificated head teacher (an essential pre-requisite for qualifying for a grant) or whose premises did not meet government standards, remained outside the system and were, therefore, not required to maintain a log. For this reason while some schools have records dating from 1862/63, others may commence several years later, when the schools were able to meet state requirements.

LOCATION AND FORMAT
Log books are normally found either at the school itself, if that still exists, or at the county record office. Occasionally, in the case of larger towns, they may be deposited in a local history library.

The Revised Code of 1862 laid down strict rules as to how the logs were to be kept. Each was to be written up in a 'stoutly bound' volume containing 'not less than 500 ruled pages'. Initially entries were to be made daily, but from the

New Code of 1871 weekly entries were accepted. The head teacher was required to make the

> briefest entry which will suffice to specify either ordinary progress, or whatever other fact concerning the school or its teachers, such as the dates of withdrawals, commencements of duty, cautions, illness, &c., may require to be referred to at a future time, or may otherwise deserve to be recorded.

An entry, once made, could not be removed or altered except by the addition of a fresh entry, and there was a firm stipulation that 'no reflections or opinions of a general character' were to be entered. Fortunately a number of heads, especially the disillusioned and the despairing, ignored this prohibition. Among them was the mistress of Hittisleigh school, Devon, who wrote bitterly in 1893 after a brush with Her Majesty's Inspector: 'One always feels that the fate of a whole year's work may hang on the humour or caprice, and absolutely on the stroke of a pen, of some Assistant Inspector'.

When HM Inspector paid his annual visit to the school to conduct examinations in reading, writing and arithmetic, plus needlework for the girls (and from the later 1860s in other subjects), he checked the log book to ensure that it was properly maintained. He also recorded in it the names and status of the teaching staff. Later a summary of his general report would be copied into the log by the secretary of the managers.

The detailed instructions given reflected the bureaucratic nature of the Code itself. However, even the Education Department recognised that it might be difficult for teachers to make interesting comments on every school day. Hence on 20 November 1862, the secretary to the Department wrote to heads suggesting encouragingly that a 'zealous and intelligent teacher' would not be at a loss to make useful and constructive entries, and would

> not find that the term 'ordinary progress' expresses the whole of his experience from year's end to year's end ... A teacher who performs this duty simply, regularly, and with discrimination, will find it a powerful help in mastering his profession, as well as an honourable monument of his labours.

CONTENTS AND USES

Many entries in the log books are concerned with pupils' academic progress, particularly in preparation for the all-important annual visit by HM Inspector. The amount of government grant received by the school depended on the result of the examinations then conducted and upon the attendance levels of the pupils. Details of disciplinary problems and teaching methods are also provided, with much emphasis on rote learning. Information is given on the text-books used, the songs learned, and the poetry recited. In some schools where there were generous patrons, prizes would be offered to those pupils who achieved the best results in the examinations or who recorded the highest number of attendances. The effects of bad weather, sickness, and child employment in reducing attendances are likewise noted.

In rural areas the seasonal employment of children in agriculture was reflected in the special holidays which were granted for haymaking, harvest, fruit picking and hopping. Schools in the poorer districts of London were also affected by the annual migrations of parents and children to the Kentish hop-gardens. 'Twenty-eight of the boys are hop-picking, and seven are home through epidemic sickness', noted the headmaster of Senrab Street Boys' School, Stepney, at the end of August 1908.

The logs indicate the youthfulness and relative inexperience of many school staffs. At St Clement's Boys' School, Liverpool, the teachers in 1862 comprised one adult male head and five trainees; three of these were formally apprenticed pupil teachers in the age range thirteen to eighteen and two were stipendiary monitors aged between thirteen and seventeen.

During the later Victorian and Edwardian period growing concern for child welfare led to the establishment of charitable schemes to provide school meals in some areas. 'Lady Jeune's winter dinners commenced this morning', wrote the head of Newcastle Street Girls' School, London, on 5 December 1894. '85 children availed themselves of the benefit — a large number had to be refused. The poverty in the school is very great, so many parents absolutely without any means of keeping their children in food'. Medical examinations of pupils are mentioned in a number of log books, especially after the setting up of the school medical service from 1907.

During the 1890s, as the rigidities of the old 'Code' system of instruction weakened, a broader approach to education can be discerned, with youngsters taken on excursions or encouraged to collect specimens for a school museum and given classes in gardening. In order to promote thrift, some schools set up penny banks or savings clubs, while others, with government encouragement, promoted temperance through lectures and the influence of the Band of Hope. Enthusiasm to promote moral and spiritual improvement was widely demonstrated, as at a Macclesfield school in 1868: 'Gave a lesson this afternoon ... on the "hog" — with the object of impressing upon the boys the moral lessons of good behaviour, cleanliness &c.'.

Log books provide much valuable information on the wider community. Entries concerning the irregular attendance of scholars often mention the need for children to work in order to supplement family income. In industrial areas, where children between eight and thirteen (or from the 1870s, ten and thirteen) were allowed to work on a half-time basis in factories and workshops, there are comments on employers' attitude to this. Difficulties in collecting school fees (or 'pence') before these were abolished in most elementary schools from 1891, further underlined family poverty or, on occasion, parents' indifference towards the schooling of their offspring.

Communal events, including fetes, fairs, sporting fixtures, and military parades are frequently mentioned, together with national celebrations like royal jubilees and coronations or successes in war. The emphasis on patriotism and imperialism in Britain at the end of the nineteenth century, particularly around the time of the Boer war, is reflected in log book entries concerning the introduction of 'military drill' into the curriculum and the celebration of Empire

Day on a widening scale from about 1904. At St. Silas's Boys' School, Bristol, Empire Day celebrations in 1909 included 'trooping the colours', singing hymns and saluting the Union flag.

Religious rivalries, especially between Anglicans and Nonconformists, and racial difficulties, for example as a result of Jewish immigration from Eastern Europe into parts of London in the late nineteenth century, are indicated in log book entries in some areas. They suggest underlying community tensions which may merit further investigation. The frequent mentions of weather conditions similarly make the books a mine of information for meteorologists.

By referring to population census returns between 1861 and 1891 it is possible to identify some of the teachers, pupils, parents and employers mentioned in the logs. In this way researchers can gain important perspectives on family and community life as well as on the education of the bulk of the nation's children.

BIBLIOGRAPHY

Ball, Nancy, *Educating the People. A Documentary History of Elementary Schooling in England 1840-1870* (1983)

Horn, Pamela, *The Victorian and Edwardian Schoolchild* (Gloucester, 1989)

Horn, Pamela (ed) *Village Education in Nineteenth-Century Oxfordshire. The Whitchurch School Log Book (1868-93) and Other Documents* (Oxfordshire Record Society, vol 51, 1979)

Hurt, John, *Elementary Schooling and the Working Classes 1860-1918* (1979)

Nash, Gerallt D, *Victorian School-days in Wales* (Cardiff, 1991)

Sellman, Roger R, *Devon Village Schools in the Nineteenth Century* (Newton Abbot, 1967)

Sturt, Mary, *The Education of the People* (1967) especially Chapter 13.

The 1851 Religious Census

J.A. Vickers

THE CIRCUMSTANCES

The first half of the 19th century saw the development of social statistics and of surveys dealing with many aspects of national life. During this same period government intervention in the affairs of the Established Church steadily increased. Parliamentary legislation sought to eradicate pluralism, absenteeism etc., and funds were made available to support the building of new churches in response to the growth and shift of population. The 'Oxford Movement' of the 1830s was in part a reaction against what was seen as unwarranted intrusion in the Church's affairs and a threat to its autonomy.

In 1851, it was proposed to widen the scope of the decennial population census by including questions about the religious affiliation of each household. A religious census had been carried out in Ireland in 1834, but in England there was immediate and vigorous opposition, led in the Lords by the Bishops of Oxford ('Soapy Sam' Wilberforce) and Salisbury. As a result, the proposal was dropped in favour of a census of *places of worship* which took place on 30th March, the Sunday nearest Census Day.

THE SCOPE OF THE CENSUS

The survey covered England and Wales. (A similar census was carried out in Scotland, the results being summarized in a Parliamentary Paper.) Separate forms were designed for Anglican and for Nonconformist congregations (the latter embracing Roman Catholics, Latter-Day Saints etc., as well as the older dissenting bodies and Methodists; also a few Jewish synagogues). A third form, distributed to Quaker meetings, asked for floor area instead of sittings. The two main types of information asked for were (a) the amount of available accommodation ('appropriated' and 'free', though these terms were not defined and caused some confusion), and (b) attendances at each service on 30th March (either the actual numbers or estimated averages over recent months) plus the number of 'Sunday Scholars'.

In the case of a building erected since lst January 1800 the date of erection was asked for, together with its cost and how the money was raised. Anglican clergy were asked about endowments and other sources of income (though many ignored this question or argued that the information was already available from more reliable sources). Non-Anglicans were asked whether their place of worship was 'a separate and entire building' and was used exclusively as a place of worship. There was also a space for 'Remarks', though few made use of it.

Returns were obtained by one means or another for virtually all Anglican places of worship, despite the fact that some clergy protested by refusing to make any response. Others submitted a return containing little or no information. Coverage of other denominations was much less complete: it has been calculated that up to 7% of Nonconformist congregations (notably, small cottage meetings) may have been overlooked. In the absence of a return, or where returns gave no attendance figures, either actual or average, or no information on the available seating, local enumerators obtained what figures they could from other sources. Some enquiries were still being pursued up to eighteen months later, but some gaps remained.

THE RESULT OF THE CENSUS

The returns were tabulated by the Registrar General's office under the supervision of a young solicitor, Horace Mann, and the results were published in 1854 as one volume of the Census Report. This contains statistical tables summarizing the figures for each denomination at national, regional, county and registration district levels. For individual places of worship the original returns, now in the Public Record Office at Kew (HO 129) have to be consulted, but those for a few Districts (e.g. Halifax, Stockport and central Bristol), like the ones for Scotland, have not survived. The returns for a number of counties have been published. (To date, these are: Bedfordshire, Buckinghamshire, Derbyshire, Devon, Hampshire, Hertfordshire, Lincolnshire, Nottinghamshire, Oxfordshire and Sussex; and Wales.)

A proposal to repeat the religious census in 1861 raised sufficient protest for it to be dropped, and, despite repeated proposals, no further attempt at national level has ever been made. (Unofficial 'censuses' later in the century, e.g. by the journalist Andrew Mearns in 1881 and a survey of London church life published by R Mudie Smith in 1904, were limited in scope. More recent surveys of church attendance at national level have been unofficial ones.) The 1851 census, despite its limitations, remains a unique event, unrivalled as a nationwide source of information on religious practice in the mid-nineteenth century.

THE RESULTING PICTURE

Out of a population of nearly 18 million, a total of 7,261,032 attendances (or 40.5 %) were reported. But Mann estimated that 30% of the population (small children, the elderly, sick etc.) were 'legitimate' absentees, and on that basis the total attendances rose to 57.9%, a figure much reduced when multiple attendances by some individuals were allowed for. More significant than any raw totals was the marked difference between attendance levels in different parts of the country, and most notably the discrepancy between urban and rural areas. It became clear that the population shift had left many urban dwellers, especially among the working classes, unchurched; but the problem went much deeper than the need for more church buildings.

At national level the figures were most significant when expressed in terms of denominational shares of the total attendances, especially if the different times of day are taken into account. These may be roughly summarized as follows:

Morning: Anglican, 54%; Nonconformist, 39%; Roman Catholic: 5%
Afternoon: Anglican, 58%; Nonconformist, 38%; Roman Catholic, 2%
Evening: Anglican, 27%; Nonconformist, 67%; Roman Catholic, 2%
Overall: Anglican, 47%; Nonconformist, 47%; Roman Catholic, 4%
               Other sects, 2%

From the perspective of the late 20th century, these figures, however manipulated or interpreted, look impressively high. But to the church leaders of a period in which England was still thought of as a 'Christian nation', the high level of absenteeism was alarming. All denominations redoubled their efforts to convert, or at the very least recruit, the pagans in their midst. But there is little ground for believing that, even in the heyday of Victorian respectability, the trends already visible in 1851 were effectively reversed. At a more intellectual level, it was, in Alec Vidler's words, an age of 'religious seriousness [rather] than of faith', with a subterranean 'turmoil of doubt and uncertainty'. And the working classes remained largely estranged.

Anglicans were particularly concerned that the Nonconformists (who had been steadily gaining ground during the first half of the century) claimed almost as many attendances, or even slightly more (according to the basis of comparison: see below) as the Established Church. So another effect of the census was to raise the temperature of ecclesiastical politics and the demand for disestablishment.

PROBLEMS OF INTERPRETATION

Once the census had been conducted, opposition gave place to criticism of its accuracy and reliability and the charge that its findings were misleading. Since 1951, when the original returns became available, there has been a steady flow of scholarly discussion and evaluation. Problems of interpretation remain, especially in relation to attendance figures. For example, it proved impossible to separate out adults and children in the congregation, despite the column provided for 'Sunday Scholars'. The typicality of the attendance figures was also challenged. Inclement weather, widespread illness and even the fact that it was mid-Lent Sunday were mentioned as reducing normal attendances; while there were Anglican charges that Nonconformist congregations had been deliberately and unfairly 'packed' for the occasion. The widespread occurrence of rounded figures suggests that many returns were based on inspired (or optimistic) guesses rather than on an actual headcount.

More important, there was, and still is, no way of determining how many worshippers attended more than one service on the day, and therefore what was the overall number of churchgoers. The official formula applied was: morning attendance + half the afternoon attendance + one third of the evening attendance = total number of individual attenders; but this was quickly condemned as unfair by Nonconformists, whose evening service was usually the best attended of the day. One alternative would be to take the highest attendance at each place of worship and add to it half the second best and one third of the lowest attendance (if any).

For purposes of comparison, a more objective figure is that of total attendances. This ignores the factor of double attenders and also the evidence that Nonconformists were (so it was claimed) more likely than Anglicans to attend more than one service during the day. A further complicating factor was the occurrence of cross-denominational attendance.

In recent years, more sophisticated formulae have been devised in order to estimate relative denominational strengths or to compare one area or region with another. W S F Pickering preferred the largest attendance, irrespective of the time of day, as giving the minimum number (the so-called 'maximum–minimum') of churchgoers on that Sunday. K S Inglis devised an 'index of attendance' in which total attendances (the 'hypothetical maximum') are expressed as a percentage of the population in any given area. B I Coleman in his survey of southern England converts the hypothetical maximum figures into a 'percentage share' for each of the main denominational groups.

One problem here is that denominations were not always accurately identified. The main Methodist denominations (including the 'Bible Christians') were for the most part carefully differentiated (though Wesleyan totals were inflated by the erroneous inclusion of some Wesleyan Reform figures, and 'Independent Methodist' congregations sometimes found themselves classified as Independents - i.e. Congregationalists). But no distinction at all was made between 'General' and 'Strict and Particular' Baptists; and the line between Presbyterian and Unitarian congregations was inevitably blurred.

ITS HISTORICAL VALUE

Whatever the shortcomings of the published Report and the difficulties of interpreting the findings of the census, its data is unique in its comprehensive coverage. Its overall reliability is only marginally affected by such factors as the varying methods of 'counting', levels of competence or trustworthiness of those who made the returns, and the number of returns completed retrospectively by local enumerators.

The original returns offer a wealth of information to local historians. They are filed under registration districts, and within each of these, under parishes. Anglican returns precede those of other denominations. Inaccurate calculations occur and were not always corrected by the enumerators. The data for other adjacent parishes - perhaps for the whole registration district - should always be examined for comparison and the local situation set against the national figures. Relatively few congregations seem to have been missed, despite the incidence of Anglican non–collaboration (probably with episcopal encouragement) noted above and the overlooking of some smaller house groups.

BIBLIOGRAPHY

Burg, Judith (ed), *Religion in Hertfordshire 1847-1851* (Hertfordshire Record Society, Vol XI, 1995)

Coleman, B I, 'Southern England in the Census of Religious Worship, 1851', in *Southern History*, 1983, pp.154-88.

Ell, P S and Slater, T R, 'The Religious Census of 1851: A Computer-mapped Survey of the Church of England', in *Journal of Historical Geography*, 1994, pp.44-61.

Field, Clive D, 'The 1851 religious census of Great Britain: a bibliographical guide for local and regional historians', in *The Local Historian, Vol. 27* (November 1997).

Gay, John D, *The Geography of Religion in England* (1971).

Inglis, K S, 'Patterns of Religious Worship in 1851', in *The Journal of Ecclesiastical History*, 1960, pp.74-86.

Pickering, W S F, 'The 1851 Religious Census — a useless experiment?' in *British Journal of Sociology*, 1967, pp.382-407.

Snell, K M D, *Church and Chapel in the North Midlands: Religious Observance in the Nineteenth Century* (1991).

Thompson, David M, 'The 1851 Religious Census: problems and possibilities', in *Victorian Studies*, 1967, pp.87-97.

Thompson, David M, 'The Religious Census of 1851' in Richard Lawton (ed.), *The Census and Social Structure* (1978).

Coroners' Inquest Records

Jean A Cole and Colin D Rogers

William Clayssh feloniously killed John Beredon at Morchard Bishop on Friday the 26th June 1355. John Clayssh accused of harbouring William after the felony pleads that William on the 29th June 1355 at the Church of Saints Peter and Paul before Thomas Scora one of the King's coroners for Somerset abjured the realm and was given a safe conduct to the port of Sandwich and that he is not guilty of harbouring him. Jury return verdict of not guilty and he is discharged.

(Public Record Office, J1/1/192)

High Court of the Admiralty inquests on convicts on board ships in Portsmouth harbour and Spithead: 18 February 1823 on board HM Racoon, George Morrison, convict, from 2 January 1823 to 17 February 1823 - Pulmonary Phthisis. Verdict: Visitation of God.

(Public Record Office, HCA1/104)

ORIGIN

Coroners were officers of the realm and were mentioned in a charter of 925 but it was not until 1194 that county coroners were established in England. Since that date it has been the duty of coroners to investigate the circumstances of unnatural, sudden or suspicious deaths, and of deaths in prison. The medieval coroners enjoyed a relatively high social standing and financial importance; apart from holding inquests on dead bodies they received felons' abjurations of the realm, heard felons' appeals and promulgated outlawries in the county court.

From the fourteenth century their status and functions declined, so that by Tudor times their chief duties were confined to holding inquests on persons who had died in doubtful circumstances and to the committal for trial at Assizes of any person against whom the jury at inquest had returned a verdict of murder or manslaughter. Coroners also held inquests in cases of fatal fires and occasionally an inquest was concerned with the ownership of treasure trove. The coroner executed writs in cases where the sheriff was a party to the suit and was also responsible for proclamations concerning outlawry in the county court.

Most coroners were elected by the freeholders of the county until the Local Government Act of1888; since then they have been appointed by local authorities. Theoretically their jurisdiction covered a whole county. Until 1926 they were not required to have either medical or legal qualifications. In much of the nineteenth century many coroners discharged their duties imperfectly; their principal defect was the frequent failure to require a careful autopsy or even any autopsy at all, and as a result the medical evidence was often lacking or at least deficient.

Some twenty towns are known to have had charters granting the right to a special coroner by 1300. In the City of London the duties were shared between the two sheriffs and a royal official known as the King's Chamberlain; early in the fourteenth century the latter was superseded by the King's Butler. After several earlier attempts the City secured a charter from Edward IV in 1478, giving it the right to elect its own coroner. The Corporation of the City of London also acquired the right to appoint the coroner for the borough of Southwark in 1550 and the two appointments were usually held by the same person until 1832.

Coroners were authorised to accept certain fees from 1487 and these payments were extended by later legislation. By the middle of the eighteenth century accounts of expenses and fees for inquests appear regularly in the account books of the Court of Quarter Sessions. Payment for such expenses out of the rates was regularised in 1752; from that day coroners were allowed £1 for every inquest held outside gaols and 9d [4p] per mile for the journey from their home to the body, provided that the place where the body was found contributed to the county rates. Their fee for holding inquests in gaols could not exceed £1. The Municipal Corporations Act of 1835 extended this system of payment to boroughs, with some modifications. Magistrates had the right to question, or even refuse, the coroners' claims for fees. In 1836 funds were authorised for medical post-mortems and in 1860 county coroners became salaried officials, in lieu of fees and allowances.

Before 1846 a deodand ('given to God') was demanded, whereby the object causing the death was forfeited to the king, the church, the immediate dependants of the victim, sold for the benefit of the poor or given to the lord of the manor. In 1800 Thomas Andrews was killed when the rear wheel of a wagon accidentally fell on his head, fracturing his skull. The wheel was valued at 1/ [5p], which the owner of the wagon paid to Lord Ailesbury as grantee of the crown of the manor of Mildenhall.

An Act of 1843 allowed county coroners to appoint deputies, subject to the approval of the Lord Chancellor, and a duplicate of the appointment had to be sent to the Clerk of the Peace. The Coroners' Act of 1887 made the appointment of a deputy coroner mandatory.

Cases are now referred to a coroner when no doctor treated the deceased during the last illness; when the attending doctor did not see the patient within fourteen days before death, or after death; when the death occurred during an operation or before recovery from the effects of an anaesthetic; when death was sudden and unexplained or attended by suspicious circumstances; or when the death might be due to an industrial injury or disease, or to accident, violence, neglect or abortion, or to any kind of poisoning.

Until 1926 all inquests were held with a jury, varying in number from 12 to 24; this was reduced to between seven and eleven but in practice many were held without a jury at all. Inquests are held in public unless there is a threat to national security, and reports have appeared in national and local newspapers for over 200 years. In general it is more likely that a newspaper report will survive than a coroner's record during the hundred years before the second world war. 'Properly interested persons' can question witnesses and see (or purchase copies of) the notes later.

With marine deaths it was necessary for a body to be produced before an inquest could be held, although in some cases when it was necessary for an estate or will to be finalised, the coroner may have held an open inquest.

LOCATION AND ACCESS.

Coroners' inquest records are public records under the terms of the Public Records Act 1958; they are normally open to public inspection after 75 years. In practice, however, many will not survive that long: after 15 years some records can be weeded by the individual coroner but certain classes must be kept permanently, such as indexed registers of reported deaths and all documents dated before 1875. Once the records are five years old they may be transferred to a repository designated by the Lord Chancellor and should be transferred before they are 30 years old. Designated offices for this purpose are county and other local authority record offices.

There are other coroners' records in the Public Record Office, most of them in the Court of King's Bench or Assize Indictment classes. (Further details will be found in the Gibson *Guide* listed in the bibliography.)

There is an almost complete set of coroners' records for the City of London from 1788 to 1984 and for Southwark from 1788 to 1932, together with some records dating back to the thirteenth century. Westminster Abbey also has a fine set of inquests for the City and Liberty of Westminster.

ANCILLARY RECORDS

Newspapers have already been referred to as important, though flawed, sources for information on inquests. The records of the Court of Quarter Sessions will also include information. Parish constables' accounts are another source (see *Guide* no 26): the constable had to gather together the jury and the costs of refreshments and other expenses will be found. Occasional letters and certificates may be found among inquisition papers and books. Burial records may record whether an inquest was held and death certificates, from the beginning of civil registration in 1837, should state if an inquest took place.

USE

Coroners' inquest records are obviously of major importance in any study of sudden death, whether accidental or not. The wealth of detail (some of which may be too much!) combined with contemporary newspaper reports, is of enormous interest to the family historian. Psychiatrists and sociologists may also find material of interest. The more modern records for London have been used for a study of the incidence of heart disease and for a study of suicide in Victorian and Edwardian England.

BIBLIOGRAPHY

Burton, J D K, Chambers, D.R. & Gill, P.S., *Coroners' Inquiries* (1985)

Cole, J A [Ed], *Coroners' Records of a Borough: Marlborough , Wiltshire, 1773 to 1835* (Wiltshire Family History Society, 1993)

Cole, J A, [Ed], *Coroners' Inquisitions for the Borough of Malmesbury, Wiltshire, 1830 to 1854* (Wiltshire Family History Society, 1994)

Cole, J A, [Ed], *Wiltshire County Coroners' Bills 1815 to 1858* (Wiltshire Family History Society, 1997)

Gibson, J & Rogers, C, *Coroners' records in England and Wales* (1988, 1989, 1997)

Gross, C *Select Cases from the Coroners' Rolls 1265 - 1413, with a brief account of the history of the office of coroner* (Selden Society 9, 1896)

Hunnisett, R F, 'The origins of the office of coroner', *Transactions of the Royal Historical Society* (5th series, no 8, 1958)

Hunnisett, R F, 'English chancery records: rolls and files', *Journal of the Society of Archivists* (vol 5, no 3, 1975)

Hunnisett, R F, *The Medieval Coroner* (1961)

Hunnisett, R F, *Wiltshire Coroners' Bills 1752 to 1796* (Wiltshire Record Society XXXVI, 1981)

Hunnisett, R F, *Sussex Coroners' Inquests 1558 to 1603* (PRO 1996)

Kellaway, W, 'The Coroner in Medieval London' in Hollaender, A E J & Kellaway, W [Ed], *Studies in London History presented to P.E.Jones* (1969)

Neal, W, *With Disastrous Consequences: London Disasters 1830 to 1917* (1992)

Sharpe, R R, [Ed], *Calendar of Coroners Rolls of the City of London 1300 - 1378* (1913)

Manorial Court Rolls

P D A Harvey

[From court roll of the rectory manor of Patrington, South Yorkshire, 9 October 1663 (Humberside County Archive Office, Beverley, PE38/Acc.1482). It was printed earlier in H E Maddock, 'Court rolls of Patrington manors', *Transactions of the East Riding Antiquarian Society*, viii (1900),pp 32-3, and is published here by kind permission of the Revd I M W Ellery, Rector of Patrington. The roll was originally written in two hands.]

Pattrington	Visus Franci Plegii cum Curia Baronis Samuelis Prowd
Rectoria	clerici domini eiusdem Manerii ibidem tentus super nonum
	diem Octobris Anno regni domini nostri Caroli secundi
	dei gratia Anglie Scocie Francie et hibernie Rex fidei
	defensor et cetera XV° Annoque domini 1663 coram Roberto
	Bethell generoso senescallo ibidem

[Patrington   View of frankpledge with court baron of Samuel Prowd,
Rectory clerk, lord of the same manor, held there on the ninth day of
October in the 15th year of the reign of our lord Charles the
second, by the grace of God king of England, Scotland, France
and Ireland, defender of the faith, etc., and in the year of our Lord
1663, before Robert Bethell, gentleman, steward there]

afferator	Ws: Story	Ric: Garner	Ric. Clapham	Rich Cocke
[affeeror]	Ws: Sandsby	Jo. Burton	Fr. Cocke	
afferator	Ws: Bilton	Tho. Dalton	Jac. Mattocke	
	Ws: Cooke	Ws: Bilton Junior	Jac. Adams	
			Juratus Tenentium [jury of tenants]	
Constable	Ws: Story			
Grave	Tho. Wykam			
Alefiner	Jac. Mattocke			

Rob. Ripley gen' for not appeareinge is Amercied vi d.

John Dawson for not appeareinge and deliveringe upp the bookes of Record as hee was impannelled foreman of the last Jury: is Amercied iii s. iiii d. [*this entry deleted*]

Tenentes [tenants]	Joh'es Dewicke gen' Juratus
	John Cheesman Juratus octob.21th

fine	The Jury doth find and present that Mr Francis Dewicke
2li 18s 6d ob.	dieed sesed of two oxgangs and thre quarters of an
[2.18s.6½d]	oxangs thre acres and a halfe and two foote more or lesse of land
	arrable meadow and pastuer and that John Dewicke is his Son

and nexte heare to the same <Copia queritur [copy sought]
15 oct. 64>

The Jurey doth present Edw: Barnard Esq for fouer Cord of	
Bursele [fence or hedge] being doune	1s 8d
and for his house being out of Repare	6 – 8d
and marck Turington for one gape liyin doune	4d
The Jurey doth present James Adam for not giveing weight	
of bread	0 – 6d
and George Boone for not giveing asise of alle [ale]	0 – 6d
The Jurey doth present James Mattocke for his mannor	
[manure] leynng in the streat	4d
and marcke Turington for the like	4d
The Jurey doth present Edw Barnard Esq fo one sure [sewer]	
being ounedun	4d

[There follow the jurors' signatures]

ORIGIN AND DESCRIPTION

Manorial court rolls are the principal record of proceedings in manorial courts in England and Wales; these courts were normally held by the steward or seneschal, appointed by the lord of the manor. The earliest original roll to survive dates from 1246, though details of some manorial courts earlier in the thirteenth century are preserved on manorial accounts, and we have extracts from manorial court rolls from 1237 and a copy of a complete roll of 1239-40. In some places manorial court rolls continue to be made as current records, for a very few manorial courts are still held.

In medieval England the administrative units of any landed estate, large or small, were known as manors; the lord of any manor could hold there a manorial court and could compel all his local tenants to attend, whether they were freemen or villeins. A free tenant of a manor might have a substantial holding with sub-tenants of his own; this too might be known as a manor and he too could hold a court for his tenants. There could thus be more than one layer of manorial jurisdiction. In the sixteenth century it was believed that if no court was held a property was not a manor, and that new manorial courts (and thus new manors) could not be created; but earlier a manor was simply a unit of an estate which might not even have tenants, let alone a court, and many new manors (and manorial courts) came into being in the late middle ages.

The business of the manorial court included the regulation of cropping, pasture and other aspects of local agriculture; decisions over debts and other minor disagreements between tenants; and the registration of all changes among the customary tenants (who included the villeins of the middle ages and the copyholders of later periods). These tenants could acquire or surrender their holdings only in the manorial court and were given copies of the relevant entries on the court roll. This function so dominated the business of manorial courts that the abolition of copyhold tenure by the 1922 Law of Property Act effectively ended manorial courts as well. In all these matters the law applied by the manorial court was the custom of the particular manor, locally determined by the court itself and often entered on the rolls as statements of custom or by-laws. The monetary penalties for breaches of custom were called amercements and were fixed by (usually) two of the tenants, called affeerors. This sort of jurisdiction, which could be exercised by any manorial lord, was known from the late middle ages as court baron.

However, the lords of some manors also exercised another kind of jurisdiction, known as court leet. This was by specific grant of the Crown, and it meant that within the manor the lord dealt with certain kinds of business that otherwise went to the hundred court held by the sheriff. These included: the right to try certain minor criminal cases, even (down to the fourteenth century) the right to hang a thief caught red-handed; maintaining standards of bread and ale offered for sale; and regulating frankpledge, a system, already archaic in the thirteenth century, which required all men to be in what were called tithing-groups, notionally responsible for the good behaviour of all their members. As a result the court leet as a whole was often known as a view of frankpledge.

FORM

Even more than one might expect of a type of record compiled over eight centuries, manorial court rolls vary enormously in their physical appearance, structure and content. They may be tiny scraps of parchment or paper, rolls of any size or large bound volumes. The earliest were literally rolls of parchment; successive courts of a single manor or, more often, courts of several manors held in a single circuit of the estate's steward might be sewn or filed together to form a single roll. In the sixteenth and seventeenth centuries paper drafts were often copied on to parchment rolls. In the middle ages manorial court rolls were always written in Latin, though it became increasingly common for particular entries (especially by-laws) to be in English. From 1733, under an Act of 1731, they had to be written in English throughout, but on many manors the change had been made earlier (as on the Patrington roll above, where little more than the heading is in Latin) and under the Commonwealth in the 1650s English was universal.

No rigid pattern developed in the way manorial court rolls were set out. Generally the order of entries seems to be the order in which business was done in the court itself; it is natural, therefore, that the essoins (excuses for absence) and the names of the jurors usually come first. Where there was court leet jurisdiction, its business is not necessarily separated from that of the court baron: the two might be mingled on the roll. Sometimes, however, court leet business was done only at certain sessions of the court — often just twice a year — and these might be distinguished in the headings, often by some such phrase as 'great court' or 'general court'. But there was not always that precise distinction between the two sorts of court that both the contemporary lawyer and the later historian might wish.

LOCATION

Manorial court rolls will be found in a number of places. Class SC2 (of which there is a published list) in the Public Record Office consists entirely of court rolls drawn from many sources, but there are manorial court rolls in other classes as well.There are many rolls in the British Library, especially among the Additional Charters and Rolls (listed in the printed catalogues of additions), and they are to be found in nearly all local record repositories. Many are in private hands, belonging to landowners or others who are the successors of those who were lords of manors or held manorial courts.

Because manorial records, and in particular manorial court rolls, provided the title of those who held property by copyhold, a 1924 amendment to the 1922 Act that converted this form of tenure into freehold empowered the Master of the Rolls to draw up rules for their protection. These rules still operate, making manorial court rolls and related records one of the very few sorts of historical record that are under any form of legal protection. Among the constraints imposed is a requirement to inform the Secretary of the Historical Manuscripts Commission if they pass to a new owner or if they are placed in a record repository. This information is entered in the Register of Manorial Documents, which can be consulted in the offices of the Commission (Quality House, Quality Court, Chancery Lane, London, WC2A 1HP). Manorial records cannot go outside the jurisdiction of the Master of the Rolls (i.e. outside England and Wales) without his permission.

USE

In considering the value of manorial court rolls to the historian there is a great difference between those of the mid-sixteenth century onwards and earlier rolls. The post-medieval rolls may give much information about the tenants of an estate (especially the copyholders); about local agriculture and the management of common fields before enclosure; and in certain places, particularly where the manor comprised a town or market, a great deal about trading debts and by-laws to curb all kinds of nuisance. Generally, however, the manorial court rolls are only one source among many which provide this information.

The position is very different with the medieval manorial court rolls. Some of the information they contain can be checked and supplemented by surveys and accounts if these survive from the same manor, but they are by far the most important source for most of what we know about medieval peasants, and on many points the only source of information available. Any study of rural England in the later middle ages is bound to draw on them heavily and topics on which they have yielded particularly important results include demography, social structure and relationships within the community, forms of tenure, the economy of the peasant household and the form and practice of local agriculture. On none of these topics has their potential been exhausted, and there must be many others still to be explored with their aid.

BIBLIOGRAPHY

Baildon, W P *et al* (ed) *Court Rolls of the Manor of Wakefield* (Yorkshire Archaeological Society, Record Series, 5 vols 1901-45, and Wakefield Court Roll Series, 11 vols, 1977-96)

Beckerman, J S, 'Procedural Innovation and Institutional Change in Medieval English Manorial Courts', *Law and History Review, 10* (1992), pp 197-252

Emmison, F G, *Elizabethan Life: Home, Work and Land* (Essex Record Office, Publication 69, Chelmsford, 1976), pp 197-333

Gomme, G L, *Court Rolls of Tooting Beck Manor* (London County Council, 1909)

Harvey, P D A, *Manorial Records* (British Records Association, Archives and the User no 5, 1984), pp 42-68, pl 7, 8

Harvey, P D A (ed) *Manorial Records of Cuxham, Oxfordshire, circa 1200-1359* (Historical Manuscripts Commission, Joint Publications no 23, Oxfordshire Record Society vol 50, 1976), pp 78-83, 607-709

Homans, G C, *English Villagers of the Thirteenth Century* (Cambridge, Mass, 1941)

Maitland, F W (ed) *Select Pleas in Manorial and Other Seignorial Courts* (Selden Society, vol 2, 1889)

Pugh, R B (ed) *Court Rolls of the Wiltshire Lands of Adam de Stratton* (Wiltshire Record Society, vol 24, 1970)

Razi, Z, *Life, Marriage and Death in a Medieval Parish: Economy, Society and Demography in Halesowen 1270-1400* (Cambridge, 1980)

Razi, Z, & Smith, R, (eds), *Medieval Society and the Manor Court* (Oxford, 1996)

Stuart, D, *Manorial Records: an Introduction to their Transcription and Translation* (Chichester, 1992)

Webb, S and B, *The Manor and the Borough* (London, 2 vols, 1908)

Prison Registers and Prison Hulk Records

David T Hawkings

It being considered necessary with a view of establishing the means of complete identification of Criminals convicted of Offences coming within the meaning of the first Schedule of the Habitual Criminals Act 1869, that the Commissioner of Police of the Metropolis should be furnished with a Photographic Likeness of all such Offenders I am directed by Mr Secretary Bruce to request that you will move the Court of Quarter Sessions of the County of Surrey to take such measures as may be necessary for enabling the Governor of any Prison within that jurisdiction to transmit to the Commissioner of Police within the periodical returns already ordered to be supplied a photograph of each prisoner of the class referred to. Provision is made by the sixth section of the Act for defraying expenses incurred which Mr Bruce apprehends are not likely to be great in carrying this arrangement into effect.

[Surrey Quarter Sessions order book, 9 February 1870, Surrey Record Office, ref QS2/1/83.]

GAOLS

Registers for many prisons in England and Wales are held at the Public Record Office, county record offices and other archive repositories, and by the prison service itself. The survival of these registers is somewhat random: some counties have good collections covering all the prisons which existed in the nineteenth century but other counties have no known surviving prison registers. The earliest prison registers date from the seventeenth century (see 'Location' below).

The Habitual Criminals Act of 1869 inadvertently introduced an interesting addition to the information required to be kept on prisoners. It stated that a register of all persons convicted of a crime in England (Wales is not quoted) with 'evidence of identity' should be kept in London by the Commissioner for Police for the Metropolis; the costs were to be borne by the Treasury. The words 'evidence of identity' were construed by some to mean a photographic likeness, as the Surrey example shows, and some prison registers therefore contain not only a physical description of inmates but also a photograph of each prisoner. Regrettably the survival of such early photograph albums is rare but they can be found; there is an early album for Bedford Gaol, for example, which begins in 1859.

Prison Registers and Prison Hulk Records

The written information recorded in the registers varies from county to county: some are very detailed, giving not only the name and date and place of conviction of a prisoner, but also a detailed description. Such records were kept so that an escaped prisoner could be positively identified. Marks such as scars and tattoos were often recorded, together with height, colour of hair and eyes and general build - slender, middling or stout. In rare instances the weight of the prisoner was recorded. Often the place of residence was given and very occasionally the place of birth. A few prisons have surviving 'registers of prisoners' effects'; these list the clothing the prisoner was wearing on admittance to the prison together with all his other possessions, such as handkerchief, pocket knife and watch. For example, Thomas Hartnell was admitted to Wilton Gaol in Somerset on 18 October 1853 with the following possessions: one coat, one pair of trousers, one waistcoat, one shirt, two handkerchiefs, one pair of socks, one pair of boots and one hat [Somerset Record Office, ref Q/AG(W) 16/9].

Prison journals kept by governors, medical officers and chaplains are of special interest. They contain details of the day to day events in the prison and name those prisoners who, for whatever reason, found themselves worthy of mention, such as those disciplined and the sick. The chaplains' journals contain many heart-rending accounts of the last hours of a condemned prisoner before he was 'taken into the arms of God'. There may also survive records of the educational achievements of prisoners; in the nineteenth century many, during their incarceration, were taught to read and write, and others had the opportunity to learn trade skills such as weaving, carpentry and shoemaking. Female prisoners were taught sewing, housekeeping and cooking. Regrettably there is little record of the detailed activities of individuals.

Until the Prison Act of 1877 counties were directly responsible for the upkeep of county gaols and quarter sessions records often contain references to their maintenance and control. Reports by governors can be found, listing various prisoners. Sickness in gaols was of paramount interest in the nineteenth century and many reports to quarter sessions give the names and nature of the illness of those being treated. An escape from gaol was a serious event which warranted a particularly detailed report.

Calendars of prisoners were compiled before a court hearing and listed all those persons charged with a crime. The alleged crime is given, the name of the committing magistrate, date of warrant and often the age and trade of the accused. Post-trial calendars were also drawn up, giving the outcome of the trial. The calendars name the gaol or prison holding the defendants in custody and may therefore to some extent supplement or replace prison registers. Calendars of prisoners survive for every historic county; they are often included with quarter sessions rolls but are sometimes filed separately.

Although technically debtors and bankrupts were not criminals those found guilty were nevertheless imprisoned. Many found themselves alongside convicted criminals in county gaols. In London there were several prisons maintained specifically for debtors and bankrupts, such as Fleet Prison, Marshalsea Prison and King's/Queen's Prison. By the Bankruptcy Act, 1861, bankrupts and debtors were no longer to suffer imprisonment except those who had been found guilty of debt by fraudulent means; on 1 November 1861 most imprisoned debtors were set free.

Until 1800 insane criminals were held in all gaols and no distinction was made between them and other prisoners. By an Act of 1800 felons found insane on arraignment or acquitted by reason of insanity were to be committed to asylums or madhouses.

TRANSPORTATION

As early as 1615 convicts were transported to America where they were used as bonded servants. With the Declaration of Independence in 1776 transportation ceased, resulting in overcrowded gaols in Britain. As a 'temporary' expedient disused warships (to be known as prison hulks), moored around the south coast of England, were used to house convicts. The hulks, too, became overcrowded and eventually, in 1787, convicts began to be transported to Australia. Transportation to Australia ceased in 1868; for a short time before this convicts were also transported to Bermuda and Gibraltar where they were also held on prison hulks. Before being transported the convicts kept on the hulks were used to build various establishments on shore. Some convicts died on the hulks and others served out their sentences in England and were never actually transported. Only one prison hulk, the 'Dunkirk' at Plymouth (1784-1791), held female convicts.

Prison hulks were maintained by private contractors who were also responsible for the maintenance and care of the convicts held on board. The cost of keeping these convicts in food and clothing was paid for by the Treasury and for this reason records of prison hulks can often be found among Treasury records. In order to claim payment from the Treasury the overseers of the hulks had to send in quarterly returns listing all convicts on board, giving such details as age, place of conviction and date when transferred to another hulk, or sent on board a transportation ship.

Prison hulk records are sometimes simply lists of the names of prisoners but other lists give the place and date of conviction, the name of the transportation ship and its destination in Australia. Some hulk registers also give details of sickness and others include lists of issued bedding, clothing, etc.

LOCATION

Most of the surviving prison records date from the first or second quarter of the nineteenth century. However 24 gaols have known records from before 1800; of these Fleet Prison (London), Northampton Gaol and Norwich City Gaol have records for the seventeenth century. Only five other gaols have records before 1790; Stafford (1712), King's Bench (1719), Surrey County Gaol, Newington (1737), Nottingham (1759) and Ilchester (1769). Some historic records once held by the prison service have recently been transferred to the Public Record Office.

All known prison hulk records are held by the Public Record Office and include records of hulks in Bermuda and Gibraltar; they are found in several classes of records. Records of bankrupts and debtors are held by the Public Record Office and others may be found in county record offices. Records of Broadmoor Lunatic Asylum and Bethlem Asylum are held by the Public Record Office and others remain at Broadmoor and the Bethlem Royal Hospital respectively.

A survey of all known prison registers and journals, and calendars of prisoners in the Public Record Office and elsewhere is given in the appendices to *Criminal Ancestors* by D T Hawkings.

USE OF THE RECORDS

The records of prisons contain biographical details of prisoners and are therefore of particular interest to family historians. The records however, cover a wide range of detail: the treatment of sick inmates, punishment, hangings, training, etc. Such material will therefore be of interest to the student of the criminal classes and the social historian, who will be concerned with living conditions and the effects of prison life on the inmates, both male and female.

BIBLIOGRAPHY

Adshead, J, *Prisons and Prisoners* (Longman 1845)

Babington, A, *The English Bastille: A History of Newgate Gaol and Prison Conditions in Britain 1188 to 1902* (Macdonald, 1971)

Chesterton, G L, *Revelations of Prison Life: with an Enquiry into Prison Discipline and Secondary Punishment* (2 vols 1856)

Clay, W L, *The Prison Chaplain: A Memoir of Rev John Clay* (1861)

Crofton, W, *The Criminal Classes and Their Control. Prison Treatment and its Principles.* (1868)

Dixon, W H, *The London Prisons* (Jackson and Walford, 1850)

Dorner, J, *Newgate to Tyburn* (Wayland 1972)

Du Cane, E F, *A Description of the Prison of Wormwood Scrubs with an Account of the Circumstances Attending its Erection* (1887)

Eden Hooper, W, *History of Newgate and the Old Bailey* (Underwood Press, 1935)

Hawkings, D T, *Bound for Australia* (Phillimore, Chichester, 1987)

Hawkings, D T, *Criminal Ancestors* (Alan Sutton, 1992)

Horsfall Turner, J, *Wakefield House of Correction* (Harrison and Sons, Bingley, 1904)

Howard, D L, *The English Prisons, Their Past and Future* (Methuen 1960)

Howard, J, *The State of the Prisons in England and Wales* (Warrington, 1784)

Johnson, W B, *The English Prison Hulks* (Phillimore, Chichester, 1970).

Mayhew, H & Binny, J, *The Criminal Prisons of London and Scenes of Prison Life* (Griffin, Bohn & Co, 1862)

Rhodes, A J, *Dartmoor Prison, 1806 to 1932* (The Bodley Head 1993)

Stockdale, E, 'The Bedford Gaol that John Howard Knew', (*Bedfordshire Magazine*, Summer 1973).

Stockdale, E, *A Study of Bedford Prison, 1660 to 1877* (Phillimore, Chichester, 1977)

Webb, S & B, *English Prisons Under Local Government* (Frank Cass, 1963).